NEW
POEMS

BY

BEN MAZER

The Pen & Anvil Press

BOSTON

To Vanessa Barnard

The poems in this collection were written between April 2010 and April 2013. They have appeared in the following periodicals: *The Battersea Review, The Berkeley Poetry Review, BODY, Bright Pink Mosquito, The Brooklyn Rail, Clarion, The Common, E-Verse Radio, Everyday Genius, Eyewear, Flexipress, Harvard Review, Hawai'i Review, Hobo, InterLitQ, Jacket, Nat Brut, Poetry Northeast, Riot of Perfume, The Screech Owl, Spirited,* and *Typo.*

ISBN 978-0-9821625-3-8

Design by Zachary Bos

THE PEN & ANVIL PRESS
c/o the Boston Poetry Union
30 Newbury Street, 3rd floor
Boston, Massachusetts 02216
www.penandanvil.com

Contents

Dinner Conversation

Dinner conversation. A blank slate
on which to install the empire. Josephus dreams
of decorating silk screens with battle scenes.
Arminius and Varus. Hilda and Hildegaard
turn slightly green but take it not that hard
when Harry with jet-streaked curls of Roman silver
flicks thick ashes into a samovar.
Piles of ripe fruit. How many poppy seeds
will we require to satisfy our needs.
Archie and Jughead analyse the field.
All is statistics, with a fudge sundae sealed.
Silence and talk are two different kinds of power.
"I have to work." The ruling class
wishes to suffer. The poor sit on their ass.
History and archaeology revive
fear of the gods, the instinct to take a wife.
A rich man's daughters are posted to inventories.
The visiting statesman approves of the lawn frieze.
The Botticelli bursts another spring.
It is of florentine silks that I shall sing.
This rough and tumble clan
will expire in madness to a man.
Ah, to be truly mad, that must be glorious,
to see each word as a sign and write in prose.
Lisa puts my toy football in her bra,
and then lifts up her shirt for me to see,
pink white breasts in magnolia taffeta.
My one wish, that I shall soon go blind!
To stop these visions dancing in my mind.
In my dream they thought I had stolen clothes
(books I had borrowed from the library).

The horizon is never permitted to doze.
The real shipment of gold
is emblazoned in flames for all to see.

Poem for the First Day of Spring

The vampire's coffin in Los Angeles
is kept company by an ape named Barabas.
Sunlight through the basement windows all day
projects dust motes where the ape and the coffin play.
This shadow was once a movie star, this grave
is a science experiment that the last actors crave.
Whoever comes here, Thelma or Clara or Theda,
will go in silence, paying homage to Rita.
Children come home from school, but that is all.
The lawn is trimmed, and the slate arches pall.

The March Wind

The wind in increments, ever so slowly,
pricks up its ears in the evaporate air,
and emanating round the ruined bricks
piled in the mud swirls of a winter's end,
makes its way homeward to the distant call
of walking spirits, waking with the spring.
A cornice topples, and the little life
of broken kings and the reviving earth
echoing rumours of the long extinct
and supple mountains, light streaks from the sky,
stretches and yawns, opening a prismatic eye.
The morning rustles, milkmen in their ken
allay the tossing of the sleeping town;
the flowered halls, and static telephone wires;
old magazines piled up against the hours.
The lime cliffs stand, belligerent pardoning gods,
judging the commerce, transactions of love,
that rise like mandates, textual, to heaven,
diffuse, particular in the coded clouds
dictating thoughts like myth before they happen.
Yet all pays homage to its clouded source
that moves the earth, and opens up the pits
in which shall sink the vivid, caustic lies
of nights of solitude out in stars' causeways,
troubling the sleepless with a life of dreams
that counters all the beaded instances
of earth life, cyclic anonymity;
the calendars of giants, dwarves of stations,
revive the absolute obscurity
of unrecorded, tempestuous intuition.
Darkness lies slain, the crippling winds and scarves,

curtaining watches, standing on the hours,
repel the expected visitor in his tracks,
with no assurance streaming from the panes
of the obliterated, iridescent
visages of rumours in reverse,
peopling silence with their less than voice.
The air stirs, puddles in the timbred ice
of obscure histories carried like a seed
to nothing at all, past all the junkered life
of codes and numbers, wearing a torn, tight smile,
to unlock the safe of many a kept girl,
raucous, complaining in her silk and pearls
of all the unfulfilled new promises,
biting a chocolate back into the box.
A car horn glares, and the stiff mustaches
of resolution fortify the day
with coolth of fractions of a shaded curb,
striving to be what is unknown and far
like savage natives in a caravan.
This is no land for works, heroic deeds
rampling raw regretful remonstrance
that twists and strains beneath a garden gate,
the ixions and sprouting grains of fate.
The pumps and sells and throngs
of national parkways stain the plecticon
of military absence, loved as radio;
green oxidized bronzes, meditating on
the auguries of anonymity,
lay awake in despair, to be so gently loved
by the great chorus of collegiate
dirges that rain in blues on annuals.
Each class acknowledges distinctions of
an older knowledge, savvy as the gods

who are exemplars of the now of love.
Their voices shake each episode above
the steps upon the stairs, the evening glove,
a closed car in the rain, perpetual mazes
that fill the autumns with their unbound lives.
These too alert the turrets to the tufts
of lifeless memory waning on the horizon,
turning to embrace the weightless shoves
of laughter at the desk of libraries
between the hours, in small communities.
There is no need to love again hereafter.
But where a stain reflects the wind of night
in shuttered gardens, by an ivory bench
on which are carved the names of mythic lovers,
stirring in silence, as if to not exist,
except as students fling in Honolulu
flowers in puddles, casting off a wish
that reemerges as a never met father,
in orphanages and in hospitals,
in fictional detectives, stumbling and flickering,
unspent and savory, idling vertiginous wives
predicting world trends, vapid upon the ocean,
where all is suckered in the colliding waves.
None who in windy october observe the stillness
of the village row of night's parked cars
is well exempted from the ghost marked factions
of other people, idolized prisoners
who visit houses, carrying relic shards
of regional culture but unconsciously,
and empty kitchens, boiling the aspirin
like asphalt to animate the masks of cars.

Avion, Gorrion

Avion, Gorrion.
What does this mean?
DC-3 divisible by three.
A bilingual entelechy.
When it was raining
a man stopped into the store,
emerging from the street
as the street must have been
to him, entering the store.
He asked for a book that didn't exist,
but were his questions answers
that didn't exist, but for me.
The rain grew darker, and the quiet louder,
separate from what we were here for,
veering into ideas of evenings just around the corner
like streaks of newsprint honouring the living,
promising a glitter of excited chatter
and the audible crackle of a firm reply
in a dry room where a fresh gaze amplifies
the removal of a jacket to an unlooking chair,
where a cloud shifts in the glint of an eye,
glowing and growing on embroidery flowering,
sinking into a gutter of loneliness
where everything that happens is obscured,
where darkness and silence become comforting
because familiar, locking the library
while other people rush to see a play.
Cocktails and cigarettes, warmer, more rapidly
affirm the towering city,
and yet apart from it I saw you were
in need of identifying in thin layers

in circles turning, what you were
as if some smile were rained on high above
the revelers distracted from their hearing,
looked on and looking on
in the frank moment of your naked gaze,
as if you put it in a question to me,
that I hesitating not to answer
revealed like thunder in rained on eyes.
A sudden meaning of the printed flower.

And what of
avion, Gorrion.
A bilingual entelechy.
What do the letters dispense with,
do they recall
forms or patterns of a habit
knowing for an unknown name.
I put it to you.
Do these omissions
exceed their tolerance
for identity ungroping to be blind.
Reaching like a bomb or gun
into the alert heart.
Most of history is lost.
These stories (rain-like chatter) point away from
jade and onyx halls the mind caresses
caught like a mirror in its desperation.
Fantastic corridors eight arms of Buddha
retain the silence of a sentence on.
Corridors that lead to many rooms
where nothing is known, or what is known,
enacted before, conspires discreetly
to initiate salvation

in evil, heaping plunder of trade,
glittering treasure so fabulous
it cannot be measured except in legend.
Removed rooms, if they exist.
Where yet upon the eve of some great journey
travelers share a meal in conversation
only dimly aware of being watched,
of activities their splendid host conceals,
unthreatening, unknowable,
the unknowing that pleasure itself delights in,
tasting rare delicacies of an exotic host.
Behind the surface what was never asked,
something to lose in pondering over sleep,
with the next day looking like lace over high cut glass,
in the image of a man inside a man,
impossible doubt left hanging, or erased.

And what of
avion, Gorrion.
Is there somewhere another,
architect, painter,
proficient in the classical arts,
to be forgotten, as if the age uproots
its mirror image, recalls strict languages
of the hour after dinner,
the unknowable brother.
The dents insert a slight influence
on schemes of color, on whole forms of classical music
kept in the silence of a marble sculpture,
opened only in the thin hours
before others wake.
Agreed upon
as if an entertainment

could ally the feelings
of what each keeps
in a back drawer, with scissors and paste and tape.
This is not that other
finding himself
seized in the midst
of a dying city
where all voices blur
bright in blindness,
the brushstroked paint
of an absolute color
in a small town's wake.
A clown seized in madness,
admitting and exonerating nothing.

Avion. Gorrion.
Say it again, but do not understand
the imprint of its meaning.
Cease to leave its foul importance
settling in a corner, in obscurity.
There is no need to understand or visit
what has been left behind, what cannot name itself
for fear of belying its greater importance,
stumbled on, perhaps, in the rain.

Manifesto

Spring comes, perspective splinters in the air
where no one looks, where pages closed, unread,
compete with walls and gardens, curbs, a gate,
a slant of light, massed shadows disparate,
interreflective to no one at all,
bursting the sap in the arriviste's heart,
a brittle sheet, creased, crumpled manifesto,
and memories awaken in the dead
in glints of lean, discontinuous volubility
that dries the hot air to the crinkling sea,
rises like ghosts on spring and summer nights
to deeper chatter, magnetic below the ground,
the common dwelling of hallucinated sound
(also they may sink along a wall
until the eye sees anything at all,
and the whole spectrum through a green leaf splays
just at the window, hailing all your days).
(The very wall that stops the shadow is it.)
A retired drunkard, reprobate
who stood this way, not very long ago,
watches the youth for individual signs
of what the ages taught the world to know,
and gets him drunk on his old favorite wines.
His university, where he was interred
for the duration, mingles love and patience,
remembers drinks by bombed out railway stations,
and paints a grand incitement philosophe
and redivivus with an expert hand.
The very young play Shakespeare on the green,
in an enclosed garden, pass the hours
until the evening collects its densities,

where luminous in the dark all passions harden.
Not her, not her, were very ghosts ago
who have unspooled the hours of the day.
Stand tall and walk, incalculable in grief,
through thousands of perspectives, like Moncrieff.
The broken bottles underneath the shed
revive a distant quarrel in a broken bed.
And puffs of clouds, floating like merchant ships,
decline the will the faded photograph saps.
Crevices of shadows fall between two buildings,
dowsing in shadow their fin de siecle gildings.
Time seen from far, from many vantages,
falls silent in attics, in the unopened pages,
which climb the trees, in all the youthful stages,
with histories of molasses and of tar
unspoken in the breezes where you are.
Their repetitious circling assuages
dumb histories, the Cyclops in his lair,
and by a mere reversal of misfortunes
revive the bard's significant distortions.
As who should suffer by a wrought iron rail
that up above two spinster's eyes assail.

The Snows of Yesteryear

As sweet as Shakespeare, snow fills the skies
outside as people fill the restaurant
for warmth, the fire burning before wartime.
Elbows down, look in each other's eyes
past sweaters signifying conjoinage to these clubs
where water drifting from the roof receives a resistant glance
besides its glimmering—cut to the point
past oriental figures, tablatures,
the lion's call the thumping trumpets
of spring the winter's watermark
in all the delicacy of their military splendour,
and business as usual to the crowds for the trains.
Dawn walks you home the insatiable glut of moonlight
through curtains gauze-like on the drawn out lamps,
they climb like stairs to deposit at the shelf
of consciousness
fizzling like champagne their leaning light of yearning.
They talk, the logs roll, whistle, crackle, fall . . .
into the fire of their heated huddle,
knowing the years and the moose on the wall,
like many a strutter, cluttering the same point,
yet not for us . . . peninsulas of sense
they urge us not to speak, indexes of
the outer mountain weep . . . the tears of Thor.
He takes her home and shuts the Buick door.
There is no magazine that exists to publish this
collateral obeyance to the hods
of manufacture . . . but the morning wakes
to find them stacked bright and right, in collegiate trim,
familiar in flight patterns with the passers-by,
and only a stiff mustache or stiff drink

past political irrelevance in the larger scheme,
"of our time". Yet Macy's or the La Guardia airport
compete concentrically, and yet elude
the late night bus terminal in Brattle Square,
an invitation to the Buckman Tavern . . .
(like Rhett or Scarlett) (disappearing and reappearing)
as you have leaned before a moonlit shrine . . .
in gossamer surprise, settled and distilful.
All the names slashed, and the codes of honour,
that took the hoofbeats of your horny voice,
are mixed within a dream, a Freudian wish,
and stand like bankers in the day at Harvard,
hobbled, and homely, one vast precarious din
in the ears, as texts pass for the state of knowledge,
hovering supratemporally over the universe.
Seen through the elbows, the waitress, and the goblets,
the snow . . . injudiciously spreads the laughter of yesteryear,
and the hard decisions are strawberry phosphates
of atomic fact the silver hound leaps,
while you are always ordering spaghetti . . .

Morning

We who are moderns, find no utterance
to carry on a morning breeze in March
our rooted anchorage in relative
relations to the utmost of dimension . . .

Particulars of flowers, jangling bells,
heard at the back like sunlight, like milk trucks
of another time—as who's to say they're not—
know stacks on stacks of sidewalk establishments,
or the grand entrances of stations and museums . . .

But what is compressed within the human heart
is idle like the unfolding of a cactus,
a desert's bloom . . . the zero substitute
of medical nostalgia drowned by sundown . . .
young doctors gathered round a skeleton . . .

The parks relieve the relics of provenance,
of which the ground speaks, hollow through the hills
grandmother pounded through a century . . .
Pine needles emphasize the light they block . . .
The author's doorway, lemon pie, her route . . .

I stand, finally incalculable to myself,
amid the stacks of worn out magazines,
piled dog hair, and commemorative stamps . . .
wondering who shall revive the fire of love . . .

I might say I'm not myself this morning,
perhaps that other whose full life I know . . .
dogmatic and dog-eared, unconventional . . .
a phoenix risen on the summer's thrust . . .

Cirque d'etoiles

And after all is made a frozen waste
of snow and ice, of boards and rags. . .
if I should see one spark of permanent,
one chink of blue among the wind-blown slags
approaching thus, and mirroring my surmise,
one liquid frozen permanence, your eyes. . .
should meet you at the end of time
and never end. . .
for always, even past death, you are my friend. . . .
and when at last it comes, inevitable,
that you shall sit in furs at high table
(for what other fate can one expect?)
dispensing honours, correlating plans
for every cause, for education, science. . .
what will I miss? how can I not be there?
who see you sputtering wordless in despair. . .
as I do now "miss nothing, nothing"
and to know you are some other man's
(the stupid jerk), who once had your compliance. . .
and do these things ever end? (and if so, where?)
I ask myself, and should I feel despair?
to know, to love, to know, and still not care?
in winter, spring, and summer, and in fall,
on land or sea, at any time at all,
to know that half the stars on each night shine,
the other half are in your eyes, and mine. . .
and what is there? And what, I ask, is there?
Only these hurt and wounded orbs I see
nestled against a frozen stark brick wall. . .
and there are you, and there is me,
and that is all, that is all. . .

How from this torment can I wrestle free?
I can't.... for thus is my soliloquy.
And you shall sit there serving backers tea.
And running ladies circles. Think of me...
Think of me, when like a mountainous waste
the night's long dreaming stretches to a farther coast
where nothing is familiar... two paths that may have crossed
discover what had long been past recall...
that nothing's really changed at all,
that we are here!
Here among flowering lanterns of the sea,
finite, marking each vestige of the city
with trailing steps, with wonder, and with pity!
And laugh, and never say that you feel shitty,
are one whose heart is broken, like this ditty.
And think that there is nothing there to miss.
Think "I must not miss a thing. I must not miss
the wraps, the furs, the teaspoon, or the kiss."
And end in wishes. And leave not this abyss.
For all is one, beginning as it's done.
Never forgetting this, till I am no one.
There is no formula that can forget...
these eyes pierce though ten thousand suns have set,
and will keep setting... now tuck in your head,
the blankets folded, and lay down in your bed.
And stir the stars, long after we are dead.

Tiresome Tiredness: An After Dinner Speech

Heave like a walrus, scurry like a rat,—
How did I get here? Sheriff,
who are these good people?
I pick up this thread of electricity
even not even not notwithstanding the ubiquity
of shaven rock.
Your townspeople are uppermost on my mind.
Today we have two civics, crevices
and also faltering like evening among the trees
the amenities
of power and forblent illusion.
I add this smoke of talk to these old walls.
Another, nearly dead, I need not name—
thinking kindly of us this morning in Baltimore.
You are my old friends. Put your neck in there.
Timing is not everything, until it's time.
The spectral rose of my own gravity
inhabits but does not defeat the cavity
of fame. Time's halters are in place.
I sing not only the times but also the contingents of the disgrace
of the defeatist proclivity of the anti-cavities of place.
This is a matchbook, I have inscribed
"I look forward to your good breakfast" . . .
The curtains are tight with spring this time of year.
Pound them.

You know what it's like.
It starts on Monday when you see the barber—
I see the lyre of Williamsburg last year.
Forgive me, a humble intruder.
Until I've weighed in on the people's couch,

and cracked the leather of the landscape's weather,
peonied accents and news services,
or rung the bell of any one mother's breath . . .

I stand under the spider, in cold earth;
all we are asking is what there is to give.

Architecture appeals to me. Well met.
Simplicity is virtue. The cardinal of lime
is also what marks each year, forget-me-not
creasing this collar, outside my window this morning.
Do not let me forget to sign the register.
Lancaster.

I run on a platform of tiresome tiredness.
Hello? Hello? How are you?
Rough torn pages, crayon-stained . . .
These too categorize a census.
I welcome suggestions. The castle is threadbare . . .
Conceived beneath a sign of sausages
and mountain milk. The old billygoat
has heard the ram of Europe.

Abbott and Costello were real people.
Yes is what you are thinking in your hearts.
I have also studied the secluded arts
of wimpole and steeple, and bargained with my eyes
to read the news and not exclude the sunrise.
Impoverished kettles of the Yucatan
brought me to service. One does not allude
to the matrix. Let Poe symbolize
the puzzling center. Tonight carouse
the ghosts of our first adolescent urges,

the primacy of ingenue excursis.
Lunch took away the sun.
I'll have me a suck-teat when the sun goes down,
for security purposes.
Cherries blossom on magnolia vines.
Gentlemen, rise.
It is not alarming to be so charming.
The railway depots flash with lemonade.
The porters are on smoke breaks in the shade.
Loosely there is merit that has stayed.
For wholesome gladness we have wept and prayed.
I do not magnify these album photos
to cast aspersions on a former clan,
nor measure them by standing in their armour.
Thank you so much. That will do nicely.
Throw off these bonds of tiresome tiredness.

The King

I

How often their predictable voices jostling the night air
within a scent's reach of jonquils and jasmine
and the eyes' blinded reach of the insoluable sphinx
turn ideas in themselves—a circulating zephyr—
too loudly, paradaisal and prismatic:
the silver words!—Death's stealth
relinquishes finally nothing but their motion;
British, French, Turkish, German, Arabic,
mean nothing to the eclipsing god,
their silence wrought in menacing origin,
that has no halve, killing them where they're standing.
The useless breasts, diminutive exchanges,
live in the shadow of their apocalyptic
certainty: beyond which there is nothing.

Why do the lovers speak
if not to disturb and unsettle eternal darkness?

II

The smooth figures shine
as if to reflect perpetual myriad
certainties, affirmations closed from inside.
The long halls deflect
their obsidian madness, tantalize
incognizable, implacable prophecies
unshouldering stone, imperfect and intact.
Confined within the silence of these walls.
Cracked boulders of glass

exact and exempt the traveller's surmise,
deferring to look into his eyes
with so much passion as to scorch the will.
Perpetually the unborn fulfill
his destiny, beyond which nothing lies.

III

What in the end is rain?
Conceit and grammar
fructifying to undo white space,
wall they are carried past as to efface
their going there—humid and perfume and guide;
to this endless motion are allied
the arts of the static—the ribbon and the drawer,
the car parked in the same lot as before
the rain draws past: calyx and surmise!
The water birds and the east central herds
repattern music, figures in disguise,
the orphan stays inside.
Night like an opiate drowns
a sense of waiting. All carved on one door!

IV

Think of it. Thousands of grids
that have their double not even in existence—
as if one steamy cloud of alphabet soup
hid not only birth and the father that is working
but the immemorial repeatable
vortex and mantle of the possible image:
descending so far beneath the immaculate sea
as to cast the city into its tributary,

reordering unity of the glozening sky.
Kempt here band of images that never die!
They tumble upside down, implacable grids
that wash out summer and anchor in the winter,
extend the fall into the breach of evening,
and block out night—the one eye of the gods.

V

So toward the mother, the mother of the father—
like crags of rock the sexless industry
that wordlessly prevails, and true north wind!
The tales of Beatrix Potter can't rescind
her personal secretary, the ornamental willow!
Like lashes of repentance the closed hand
leaves just one crack for the boy King to enter
past ancient sleep to crawl out on the window
and see the city spread like landing gear
where orphans close on one immaculate rose!
What came before holds steadfast like a center
behind the mind's blind decade, decadence
that even the talons of the sinless purchase!
Strangers upon the road to Troy. O boy!

VI

So late to the images let one arise—
as if without reason. Pivoting on one end—
that all the city should drain down to this,
prophetic upon a porch, lead to a kiss.
Stranger, familiar still he cannot name!
But to observe it without thinking again!
That all the city should drain down to this—

vast and remembered, throbbing without pain,
pivoting on one stranger, who foresaw!
Who had provided the prophetic porch
that ended in the procession and the torch!
Come again! This image comes and comes again—
although the boy King's mother be in Spain
or husbandless: is marked out bright and plain.

VII

And end in rain. Just as it begins.
To wade through the perpetual hieroglyphs,
one constant stranger, visiting to tea.
The afternoon sinks down: Chinee! Chinee!
And though you have a lot to say to me,
blankets the evening and conceals the night—
as if one starry fog were shining bright
to be repaid with afterthoughts. One bliss!
Sinking into an opiatic haze
as if there were no number to its days.
I can't recall! I can't recall the sights
but, as if the silent film restarts,
and has a lot to say, the broken lights
serve to remember what they cannot name.

VIII

Yet the convincing armour of the wind
concedes no victory. The castles shroud
the statuary and the hall speaks loud
of what is not regained. Love is not stained!
if it be love. It is not for the crowd
to pick through dung reserved but for the king.

It is the solo party that shall fling
the name about, cross purposed with the wind.
The coming of the age it is will find
what it possesses—that it hath one mind.
And cannot answer. Arvind! Arvind! Arvind!
Settle and possesseth of the wind
the one true beauty. Arrive and you will find
the treasure that hath left the past behind.

IX

Out there, in the backyard, out by the sand box,
a world of laundry lines runs like planets to the stars,
it is so vast a world to call across,
and steeped and drenched in promise, like those stars
paired to grow brilliantly in shining pride.

Shapes retaining the imagination,
stepping forward, without even a voice to call,
but wrinkled by the wind, as if important,
the peach trees repeating what they made the planets,
endless, but even then a legend of loss.

Are memories real, or only imagination!
The oldest memories of rooms and flags . . .
They can't have been, as this itself can't be.
All is previous! Yet joyous to live inside them.

X

How often what is apparent is only a sideshow:
dressed up elaborately in a costume of crowds
and customs, signifying walls

memory erodes, more powerful than towers of steel,
their scattered archives as transient as Atlantis!
And yet you called my name and I was there,
pinnacled at the same height of the city,
at time's perfection: emblem and ideal
two sets of eyes meet only at one time:
secret and brightest gem in Christmas' setting.
Yes, they adon the sheerest silver robes
to perch upon the equinoctal stars
and see all myths surveyed and intertwined
and point out toward what the new year will find.

XI

Then all alone, to sweep the dusty pavement
within four walls, and never to see reprieve!
Until the local minibus lets out
into vast caverns (its sudden new schedule)
of rooftops tangled by snow, sky and trees.
Matchless out here among the eternities!
As if in every direction they would climb
to know no end, but one obscurity.
This is love! To know one name and limb
squelched and silenced by the voice of god.
The driver lets another passenger inside
then you depart, aimless, unwitnessing,
here where the rooftops tumble upside down
and nothing that you think or do is known.

XII

Still see them flying, fantastic, unrestrained,
like pearls of heaven, masters of the wind,

whose flags are sheer scarfs tattered by the cold!
To rise without reference upwardly so bold
their only aim! Mild avatars of fame!
What grisly mechanisms dash them down!
And how, how, how can they still believe
the icy zenith of the wind's reprieve!
To cross as if in one magnificent X
the lofty channels of their tabooed wrecks
and still no shame, to leave us but a name,
or part of an engine that propelled their fame!
Above the heights they rise!
Shrinking our cities in their watery eyes,
their maps beyond compare!
Converging with the stars because they dare!

XIII

Harpo was also, know this, Paul Revere.
And Frankenstein, and Dracula, and Jane.
Or would you say that I have gone insane?
What would you do, then, to even the score?
And what is more, should the boy King stand clear
and leave the sword undrawn, and face the door?
I could tell you, so many times before!
How every store front is its own museum
and where we two meet in the eyes of heaven.
Traffic stop! And listen to me now!
The King has spoken, and he takes his bow.
O How! How could his little woman
be admitted to the judgement of heaven.
The judgement day is here, the day is now!

XIV

Moonlight like glass like milk like coconut milk
so far south that the pallet the mind strains
paints new predictions with or without rains
on the still obsolescent hacienda!
This double life is the very last mind bender
in an unconsidered life if it at last be born
in heirloom portraits and undiscovered silk.
What will the morning bring! For now to sleep
without escaping these promises so deep
the glass bric a brac shines with their insignia
and wheels into the dark, the vast enigma
of a life unlived—the whole world turns
and seals its secret as the man boy yearns
for his identity and figlia.

XV

No mystery if the cats gather as this strange encounter
should have come to have emblematize the city:
for of all those who passed and paid homage to their peer
only you remained, after the room was clear.
The way is unsteady, past the museum of thoughts
that jostle the aftergoers after midnight,
but the way home straight: one shot of hammering train,
then silence. You enter the unexpectedly grand
unflowering existence, emptying your hand,
and admiring the disorderly filaments,
exacerbated desires the morning must put away.
But now: the full confession to the stranger.
The night drives like a rocket to its danger,
apart from the world, and with nothing to regret.

Philip Nikolayev!—at thirty-eight.
The night before our lifetime's greatest party!
We stood outside the KGB Bar's gate
and passed a joint around. He said:
I can't remember what. I wrote it down
in a matchbook. Remember us when we're dead.
Our life was wild with surprise and with surmise
and a half-inkling that it came but once,
could come no other way. We filled the dawn's
streaky blue-red-yellow with words and weeds
on our own Hudson Bay; such were our deeds.
We were the toast of all the poets once,
and filled many rooms with much incessant laughter.
May god forgive us for what must come after.

XVII

Landis and Stephen! Discoveries in my bed!
A letter mailed at dawn. Geoffrey was gone.
Anything happened. Much synchronicity
confuses the immaculately precise.
No wonder who heaped these treasures in our eyes.
We hashed them out. In the parked car till dawn.
When every color from every shape was gone,
and all that remained was upside down in bed.
I talked the universe out of my head,
and you were my mirror. I was understood!
The poetry we wrote was more than good,
it was unreal and real. Now what we feel
descends to that world which exists beyond the grave.
Where no one sleeps, and language is our slave.

XVIII

What was her name for hours past Sather Gate
and on the bus to San Luis Obispo
she was my cell phone wife. Enchanted life!
To see once more like a great enchilada
the spread out fields down to the central coast.
Life is a dream! That trip I liked the most
where in a storm—do I really this recall?—
they burned some candles, had painted on the wall
the "Madrigal" that Landis wrote for me.
I sojourned on a remote mountain top
where nearly every cell phone call would drop,
surrounded by wolves. And lions. Good Roy Kahn
drove me through torrential rain storms at dawn
to have coffee on the isolated pier.

XIX

Skittering images! Gone with the Wind,
The Love-Ins, Charles Boyer, Irene Dunne!
The signals mixed and crossed—an afterlife
of quantum time-ash—white hairs on my head!
Eternity a headline newsprint thin,
existing nowhere! Brought this back to Berkeley,
where much as I roamed, no people did I see.
Jack Spicer's ghost! And Duncan's!
What's it to me
if these continue on and live
without a history?
My best friend died;
the winds, the pines, the redwoods are allied.
I am outside; does no one live inside?

XX

Berkeley at night. The stellar enchilada
conveys my sympathies to the oblique
and passing tragic traffic. The physique
of unoperating restaurants without a key
hides my own matic. Deeper than that I go
to where the light shields chutelike on one static
querulous quest of footing where rats go
and no one bothers, I will meet no other.
This is life without sun, without father or mother,
where I may as well have killed my brother.
Eternity stops. Beyond that what else is there?
Just me and the moon. My footsteps.
Is the world real? Do these places exist?
I hear nothing. Soon I will see nothing.

XXI

Cataclysmic simultaneity,
how they return in the moment inevitable,
too scary to face. Huge crescendo of volume
to minor subtonic, then back again, a rock cliff's face,
stark, sliding, struck by lightning, continually alternating,
unbearable revelation. Shrouded in darkness,
yet revealed. Horrible to look at. Those notes that are
what you heard are now binding. Yes, the expedition
was sent to Brazil by the British. Like Dracula or the Mummy,
they didn't even know what they'd hear. Elusive revenge
of the gods, shaking the world, on a cliff's edge,
stark (with lightning crackling, breaking the darkness).
Ancient, not to be fooled with.
Signals go out, received all over the world.

XXII

In imitation of the sun's energy—
in its capacity of a direct motor.
Forces at work in hidden corners of nature.
Turning the Gunga or the Brahmaputra,
back to its sources. View us as simple men.
"not only that They existed".
"given to Mr. Sinnett". "the Master K.H.".
Avalanche in the Karakorum Mts.
Letters will cease at her death.
Simultaneously in Tibet and Egypt,
in London and Paris, New York and San Francisco,
Los Angeles and Russia. Nearby in Peru.
Breakfast is served in the Alps.
They have written, they have written. Written. Written.

XXIII

An Old Lady in the Natural History Museum

And should the afternoon go down
upon the echo of the brown
enumeration of our race
and leaving a residual face
exempt us from this constant place
still see incognizant the sign
levelled between the smile and frown
and cropped hedge the long anodyne
and evening parallel they drown.

For there thin lips and watered eye
are hunched upon the citadel

in deep inversions of the sky
and permutations of the town
that the old crone will never tell.

XXIV

At Karnak the boy king was buried alive.
The burial party silenced. Three thousand years passed.
At the last moment of the concession to dig
the sixteen steps were discovered. The unbroken seals.
The mummy walked. Who saw it went insane.
The Lord patron died of a mosquito bite.
Ten years passed. The annual expedition
of British complained about the Cairo museum.
A stranger was found there at night, by the scrolls of Amen-Ra.
A beautiful aristocratic Egyptian woman
sleepwalked out of an international cocktail party,
was found unconscious on the steps of the Museum.
A guard was dead, and the old ageless guide
requested once again to be let inside.

XXV

How many times bungling boys from Brooklyn
will tear up the screen with their jokes and women.
Did they know Hart Crane? At evening's silver party
they are the least likely of all to go insane,
but peopling the leaves beyond the orchestra
might catch a glimpse of the heroine's golden bra,
but what of it? They're sailing out at dawn,
impersonally speculating on
the cleanest outcome for the neighborhood.
Sometimes the roughest wiseguys must do good.

An Asian don checks their progression
but at last by their concession
they occupy the ingenue's obsession.
Even the luckless smile at what they've done.

XXVI

These laundry lines lead nowhere, whipped by rain.
Perhaps each in some window survives a stain.
Impenetrable cubicles, stacked and spread out grid
fortified and multiplied by discolored brick
and blocks of concrete emptied of their makers.
The sky drifts black and blue, but no one sees
primordial origins, stark auguric trees,
pretexts of order crumbling to disorder.
Death shakes the silence that the worn heart leaves.

XXVII

Just where the east with central west aligns
I found myself alone. The cell phone lines
broke through the silence of obscuring brick
and blocks of limestone where the decades pass
unnoticed. Time's grand central coordinates!
The flowers fluttered at the first signs of spring,
and my voice drowned, an all too eager familiar.
You walked me towards you, darker and hard to see.
Had I arrived on time? You wanted me
one earlier April. Time lasts too long to be
of use to the living. Stumbling I found you.
Was it too hard to be
where everything passes, to hear you talk to me?
To ride the train home, your hand upon my knee . . .

XXVIII

for Joe Green

Saturday westerns. Munching on granola
like Leon Erroll in the Siberian wastes,
I cannot separate myself from place,
from Little Miss Marker or from Robert Newton,
the Scarlet Pimpernel with his silk suit on,
Bud Abbott shooting on a mountain side,
is home more real!
The walls are separate from what I feel
and the ceiling slides into the woods
whose sun burns in my eyes. The library
is voices that I see. I've closed the door
and uncoil like a snake upon the floor.
My mother cries! Put the books on the shelf!
You've climbed entirely into yourself!

XXIX

Why should the aged eagle spread his wing?
I'll tell you why. Because to watch Santa bring
a billion presents from the frozen pole
all by himself is less than heartening.
He brings them door to door
with Hyperborean speed. You who are converted
are harnessed to his creed though you have skirted
the issue. Who is that dark stranger?
That sickly twisted dying frozen ranger
who captivates the grove where you, too, rove.
I think he is myself! The least sure elf
mixes these patterns and brings them to the slatterns

who place them in dust till Easter on the shelf.
They call him Stetson, I have four sure bets on.

xxx

The chair she sits in like a burnished throne
happens to be the King's, and is my own.
Maybe I too descend into parody
but not without esoteric clarity.
The least sure elf
is pining to be made into his self,
but I have already explained myself.
Pure tragedy must needs be humourless
and poetry will not be cured unless
its certain tragedy is made refined.
I too among that Harbour Dawn have pined
for quintessential pure lucidity,
perceived the cortex of the trinity,
and each emotion to its word assigned.

xxxi

Manhattan in the rain. I couldn't speak
when Uncle Sid drove me in from Rockaway.
What did I want? To visit the punk rock shops.
The statue of liberty seemed oxidized and locked,
too fleeting, like shops I only saw when they were closed,
left for another lifetime. What would we have said if we talked?
Head of the Vice Squad. My mind was exploding with vice.
When I came back from England I was lost,
and sat in my Aunt's house in Far Rockaway
watching Abbott and Costello night and day,
as vacuum cleaner salesmen, rival clans,

detectives, photographers, victims of circumstance.
I pilfered the attic for Pogo and Mark Twain,
ate seven kinds of cereal (she had three sons),
and saw Mrs. Wiggs and the Cabbage Patch again.

XXXII

Words! How can I deploy a dozen at once
on top of each other, the way I might read a page
backwards and forewards, in one photographic instant,
stretching the tongue in all directions at once,
to say the unsayable, cumulative and percussive
explosions signifying an enduring silence,
one fusion of confluence and inclusion,
packed with the weight, the indivisible density,
of all remembered experience and emotion,
and fraught with primordial defiance of the linear,
stabilizing possibility in one vocable,
one sound of thesis and antithesis,
one word for everything, all words in one,
a form large enough into which to put anything!

XXXIII

Anne Britton. Why do my thoughts always come back to this?
How on the edge and outskirts of the city
high on a hill worthy of Disney, or Seuss, or Mr. Burns,
high on a hill overlooking
what seemed like all the world—
crags and crevices, shadows, and blinkering lights,
some corner where a cobweb spun, where
nobody entered, where in another world
of brick on brick, orphaned, without witnesses

perhaps an old lady—kindly and unobserved—
may have fed animals she talked to,
called names, her heirs—a mildewed carpet
byzantian and worn amid the high mantles
and rafters seen by the impossibly small.

XXXIV

Branches grow in all directions at once.
Their black silhouettes enclose
the opposite of the city that surrounds them—
even then the white air of orphanic pilgrimages.
They dine on spaghetti! The instruments measure gold!
And when in the longing that descends in darkness
they take their cue to motion
(all things are there!) what never happened slows
into familiar memory, and the winds whip
their thousand frames and borders (enticing as lace),
in cross purposes, symphonies of erasure,
expansions of dimension and perspective
extending outwards down every road and lane,
groaning and growing inward, cross hatched by the rain
(whose sudden abundance even now overflows).

XXXV

Spring nights in high school—some legend revealed
as far as all the laundry lines could take you
through a universe of backyards, to a distant and returning star.
Like a cock's crow plunging beneath the planets
to the mythic origins of what we are.
Revealed! So in celebration we circled
the little town, for all lines are a circle,

coming and going the same, till you grow tall
and strong, worthy of bearing a name:
like shrouds of darkness the points we pierced
with our individual lights, passing and hailing like stars,
until all was uncovered, each one knew each one,
the circle completed, a simultaneity
of all points from A to D to Z.

XXXVI

for Isabel Biderman

Finally to see with eyes of onyx and jade—
what's always there. Cleopatra with her crown
gives O's for X's, gives X's for O's
perpetually working towards the city's center
by katty-corner, wishes too grand to grant
—for who can both live in the rarest palace
and be its guest? Passing again and again
brings nothing closer—a few feet in the end
and all is different. Different and the same!
A better life, taller and rising to heaven
(the dog escapes, returns according to plan).
Fabulous laughter lives in the hereafter.
The cat withdraws into its impregnable dream.
The actor leaving the palace is just a man.

XXXVII

Each is the same, each different and the same.
The most fabulous windows let three sets of eyes
aligned at Christmas, at the center of the world,
admire its fusion of the past and future,

one after another, converting pleasure from pain,
in endless profusion, each image containing each image,
imponderably long, too long for the eyes to sustain
for its duration: faith and hope and renewal!
The makers of the world gather each jewel
with humour and innovation
and admiration of the classic forms
defying dispersion: and glittering with grace!
Mapping with silver and pearls the planets in space!
Each, one by one, her pilgrimage to that place.

XXXVIII

The motors roar! No calendars erase
each different corner that they signify,
though each is drenched in darkness! And perfumes,
like vintage draughts and plumage that caress
the mind's thumbprint-tip, periscope windowscapes
elapsing into silence, gone too fast.
Where they remain—as if ever they stood
imagination to its single undrinkable clasp
in primitive tribal echoes no word can grasp
except as a hieroglyph—untested, real,—
are only verified in what we feel
we know, so staggeringly slow
they speed up till they are backwards before they go,
in pillowed images, stung by the asp.

XXXIX

You might have been anyone. Your relatives anyone.
The place—where were we?—might have been any place.
After dinner and talk that can only go so far

we moved beyond the doorbell as if to be understood
by going so far—no direction but to fall
in the betweenness of hours up the zig zag of streets
where no one calls and everything repeats
the insistent identityless rhythm
that is our shield and passport—unhearable beats
seeking the eternal and lost child.
Unanswerable and hung up on a star
like all the nights we died anonymous
moving dead leaves like beads across the wind,
retiring all our talk in the monstrous dark.

XXXX

In the garden the night is directionless,
the wind one wind, unfathomably far
and relinquishing time in its shrill precipice.
The flowers stand and shine, returning no images.
From what corner have they come,
standing sentry apart from all the sleepers,
as if one permanent incognizable sign
to be read in the cosmos for an eternity.
The basement casements, dusty with disuse,
convey with their impregnably abstruse
recalcitrance an inner life, to all
who are among the living of no use.
The wide walkways of the stars divide
chapters of our lives like music in reverse.

XXXXI

These inner courtyards frame at least as well
the towering cognizances like a sea of soup

that hem in all that you can never tell.
The bricks besplatter clatter, drown and droop
in the time's eye that waits too long for you
who betoken all that you have to do
and still surmise the patchwork of the skies
that spanks all basketballs and infancies
where the brick prisons rise and the trees trough
the fog as if it couldn't get enough
of being, and where you look as of surprise!
Retired on night busses these secrets doff
their caps, and settling their feet up
look westward upon each immaculate roof
as if it might be home. Drink from this cup.

Entering the City of New York

Entering the city of New York,
is something like approaching ancient Rome,
to see the living people crawling forth,
each pipe and wire, window, brick, and home.

The times are sagging, and it is unreal
to know one's slice of mortal transient time.
We angle forward, stunned by what we feel,
like insects, incognizant of every crime.

We are so duped, who make up civilization
in images of emotions that we feel,
to know the ague of the mortal steel,
each one perched balanced at his separate station.

The graves are many, and their fields decay,
where nothing can be meant to stand forever.
No doubt in due course God will have his way,
and slowly, slowly, all our bonds dissever.

But we shall not be here to see it happen;
we will have left this world behind to others;
there is no silent power who is mapping
our hearts and wishes, or those of our brothers.

Lift high the head, and let the jaunty scarf
blow in the reckless wind of each new morning;
walk to the edge of each old well-used wharf
and see imprinted there time's towering warning.

See with fresh eyes the little that we are,
the stump, the shattered window, and time's scar;
beating your chest, exult to have come so far;
stand at the edge of time's still promontory,
accepting your role in the unwritten story,
where lethe-wards we travel in the dory
of each borrowed, rented, dented car.

The lives are many, and the riches few,
though somewhere they are fabulously piled,
as useless to the living man as to
forgotten kings through whose fingers they have filed.

Particulars of prowess, social standing,
all equally must face God's reprimanding,
until all stretches out in endless sands,
and each no longer knows his lover's hands.

The cantors and the funerals have plied
their rituals in small communities,
each like the many others that precede it,
poor orphans of the storm, we must concede it.

Delicatessens all are richly piled
with meats and cheeses, treasures, delicacies;
each generation goes, but all are styled
upon the blueprints of established keys.

Impoverished lovers huddled in the doorways,
of ancient carvings and dishonoured brick,
all have their fabled, tragically real stories,
exalted till time exerts its famous prick.

The painted lover in his walled-in room
must pace and fret, exerting to be known
the meagre wishes that he calls his own,
in sparkling breakfasts that relieve his gloom.

Stand on the kingly carvings of a coin,
and looking down, see where each crevice lies,
aloft the damp pianos, each mouldy groin
of wall and carpet's strict amenities.

And when the night takes cover, letting in
a maelstrom of resurgences, begin
to lengthen prospects of a shadow ghost
of gestures, particulars where you have been!

An alley narrows to a drop of rain
that knows no patron but the valent skin
of shoe-wet footsteps, brave beyond all pain;
without a name then, let your life begin.

With Caligari at Octoberfest,
and on into the night, where wind-spires send
unopened messages to scattered streets
toward which our passions shall unfettered bend!

These spectral certainties have no clear end,
although they are not mapped, but constancies
of one ghost city, upon which we attend,
exult to hold us steady, mobile in their seas!

And into ladies parlours, balls defunct,
the presence hounds the night and jars the shutters,

exempting no absence or childhood spent half-bunked,
seeking that other who at the top opera stair utters!

For there, for there, at the top opera stair. . .
one perfect innocence exuding stars
that join the heavens, violet and dense,
lies at the heart of love that truly matters!

In an unopened box, these presents rest,
meant for some other fortune has more blessed;
for now, let all desire overcome
with sleep, nurture, solidify love's kingdom!

In zig zag byways of the shopworn heart,
each one extends his own ghost-flooded streams,
makes tribute to traditions he will own
until the many faces all must marry
impalpably the universal mart,
to be reborn in some late other's dreams!

A Dream

I was the last to understand
what she had never understood.
How Washington and Talleyrand
had made her sad to make her good.
From Nashville to the Cumberland
her father owned five hundred slaves
who grew tobacco on the land.
God bless the innocence of knaves.
I met her on a dark strange night
in Clarksville, in a gothic manse.
And knew that nothing had been right,
for too much had been left to chance.
The child was hers, and not some man's.
She fled New Jersey, went back home.
She turned down every plea to dance,
until her tears began to come.
And talked of how they had to bury
dark secrets of the cemetary.
How on the graves young men made merry
until she had been forced to marry.
How in the morning she reviled
herself, and felt most sick.
How after the divorce was filed
no other man could do the trick.
Until she met a gentle sort,
who did not know a woman's heart.
How she consented to his court,
and made with him an honest start.
How half her daughter's mind was black
with demons, and a father's lack.
Why did she tell these things to me,

most gracious on a dark strange night
beneath a wilted, haunted tree,
in terrible, distorted light,
as if these truths were half my right?
I'll never see her kind again,
most captive in her yellow gown.
Her beauty reached from now to then.
Her smile has left me with a frown.

Broken Blossoms

An old chinese master, coiled like a snake
in a wicker basket, sits and smokes
his opium pipe—somewhere near the docks
where rain floats upward, the prisoner of silk smocks,
to be his dream, who twists the golden locks
of a nubile and itinerant girl,
who fascinates him, every curve and curl.
Although she sits at his feet,
the closest memory is the dingy street
outside their solace, where darker grays repeat
the threatening world. His nails are long and pearled.
Critical theory of the future's hurled
through muted rain, and can't survive this stain.
The world is concrete, narrow, hard, and plain.

Yet rushing to night, a hero somewhere strays
not far nearby, to serve such luck as stays
time to its chain—
and loud applause, the luckless dim refrain
of massive silence, fills the whole world's brain
to follow him, and nothing as they are.
The faceless crowds. His efforts know no gain,
the night bring on. These separate episodes
are comic in their endless finite modes.
Two solitudes converge along paved roads
to carve and quarter night. He lost the fight,
but somehow won the millionaire's esteem.
The luminous emotions tear and teem
through causeways of the night's divided fate.

Golden Boy

Up there where decision drives like an implacable wind
the division between what is desired and what is demand,
the top of the city seems suddenly explicable
and reality itself the foremost fable,
whether rich or poor, whether in or out the door.
The hand freezes brushing against hair, brushing against another,
whether a small daughter growing to be a wife and a mother,
and the insistence to fall is tearfully bitter,
to fail to succeed seems to be elaborately better.
But to convince her, who holds the key to it all,
with the double doorway of her half-cowed allegiances,
is equal to an entire lifetime of stress,
broken hands, the spurned violin, the old world father's distress,
the decision to ride by a cab to the upper side,
the stark silvery icy refusal to take a dive.
For now is now, and nothing anyone can say,
can never again take the smallest of dreams away,
whether they let him go, chalking him up as crazy,
or do him bad, stating that he is lazy.
No matter, here, now, at the top of the world,
in the massive city, undulating and whirled
on the silver spikes of hope, the beams of lights
that crush the weak, debilitate their spirits,
like shadows he sees the spirits of all his fights
fall away, knowing love in a grain of sand, in one of the world's nights.

Martha's Vineyard

1. Iconry

Electric doorframes in a void of death,
they pass their moment . . . . who can blow them back
from the flat matrix of their raw spent breath,
as if the world were black . . . . their pointillistic flaw
is mores and manners boiled down from raw awe.
Vivekananda, Dean Inge, Charles de Gaulle,
pre-Kennedy, pre-war-dead, Fillmore-fall . . . .
the foliage glistens . . . . we are what we are . . . .
lined and assigned . . . . this paper iconry
was once surveillance of a standing army.
Old news . . . . how many lifetimes do we use
to get them back, or to become like them,
ourselves . . . . to notice everything's the same,
one destiny, one root. The mind of man . . . .
We bury ourselves. Will we come again?
The staple rusts. The paper buckles, folds . . . .
catching the no-light of the nothing sun.
Curved like a breast . . . . their colors all undone.
O City, City . . . time to put away,
the Cyclops and the red wren's throbbing play.
The August slag-heaps drink anonymity,
and tick like God . . . . each garden and each clod
repeat, repeat the first trespassing feet
uttering Mary, Mary . . . . nothing stirs
that feels like man. Yes, Luce. Yes, Ciao Manhattan.

2. San Luis Obispo

First thing I learned was there had been a war.

All night I pulled the white hairs from my head
and draped them in the basket. The mirror shone
their million bright strands like the tv set
that ran in the next room, movie after movie,
light fragments sweeping without breath or death,
sharp cuts from shot to shot, from plot to plot
each time I crossed the room, figure from figure
existing nowhere—was I who I was—
to think of him, blown to ash and headline.
All night I stared in my own little terrace basement room
they gave me while they slept above all life,
my absent captain and his vacant wife,
surrounded by finery on their mountaintop,
the empty pool. Each cell phone call would drop,
for there was no connection in this section
but what I understood, alone for good.
The mirror shone, and my own face was glass
a vague wind buttressed, timelessly to pass
like the burnt match I left upon a sill.
It stifled. Brilliant colors less than real
sped on, preceding what you had to kill.

3. Old Jazz

Vintage jazz, distilled for eighty years,
still twists the needle on the turntable,
its bass and boom filling the ivy shadows,
your night-begrottoed, vine-besotted lair.
So we descend into the pure black night
of empty winds and remnant visages,
a window too high to climb, reflecting dark
nothingness, as if someone were there.
Then lower to the basement casement's glare

of spring's cold flower-bursts where long past midnight
the past shoots back its silent angry stare,
infinite and inhuman as an ocean
that waves in glass, holds our attention there
in too great detail. I hear my own words pass
into dark oceans of our listenings,
afterwards, backwards. Creeping through the hall
of someone else's directions, my dead eyes fall
on a white stone, carved there for me to see
like my own death, the simple legend "MARY".

4. Rain

The windy rains come, apposite as China,
to your low neighborhood, the cut brick streets
empty as movie sets, forgotten novels
of orphans at the precipice of travels,
and dull your sleep, while I, the wakeful child
surmise each alcove and each pediment
as if it were your past, a continuity
of nothingness preserved. The gutters flood
and river fast past where the parked cars shine
like love letters in ribbons, yours, now mine,
where the Victorian clock breaks on my heart,
where old things, never finished, have their start,
and I am one, and have done with the sun
to enter white blackness, and another time.
These meditations are confined
to photographs and legends, what they are
not ready to return to any car
where flappers still revive the laughter that
disturbs the ruffled silence where I sit.

5. Arrivals

The stacked volumes by candlelight or tv light
were artifacts of time. What the tv played:
arrivals at Oxford, repetitive and old
like shadows in a cave. I crossed the room,
eyes on the oriental carpet where I slept.
Their patterns burned under the brilliant back and forth
of light and then less light, then back again
in continuity, flashing their signals
out the windowshade upon the gray whiteness
of a city asleep, horse-trodden by a shade.
Characters composed only of light and shade,
they rode bicycles, or talked, one to another,
back and forth, in black and white, first black
then white, then black, piano keys
of hope and promise, an underworld of made
images—a blank city, a new birth.

6. Cambridge in the Seventies

I started middle school in '76,
around the corner from where Robert Lowell lived,
on Sparks Street, white haired poet about to die
at 59. Perhaps we walked by each other.
It was my introduction to Harvard Square—
the 1920s barbershop tiles at Bailey's
(where Buster Keaton must have gone in College),
Harvard Stadium where with Michael Goodman
we interviewed the quarterback Jim Kubacki,
the Radcliffe president's house where Tia Horner lived
(I tried to walk her home each day from school),
then closer to Harvard Square the Brattle Arms

where my orange-haired artist friend lived with his mother,
Oona's where we coveted Jimi Hendrix leather
imagining the sixties were thousands of years ago,
the futuristic and towering glass tunnel
connecting one part of the Harvard Coop to another
high up in the autumn turning to winter air,
repetitive images seeming to rise to heaven,
the stark black outlines of trees, my friends' houses were weird—
enormous high Victorian affairs
with dormers and bay windows and huge doorframes,
attic rooms you could bump your head on—
their single parents never seemed to be home;
and must have been permissive; razor blades,
cerulean bottles of ink, intellectual black birds
who must have personally known Timothy Leary:
slightly creepy like a drawing by Edward Gorey,
they hustled the crowds of Cambridge children in
to children's eggnog, trunks of Playboy and sheet music
(that Shakespeherian rag): Shady Hill
stood like a mirror image of who we were,
paupers and orphans somehow disaffected.
Through all of it, the feeling of something I missed,
some way the other kids were more together,
little Peanuts of the ancient-recent past.
The cool kids were jocks, or girls whose hair was feathered.
The first party that I went to we smoked grass
and listened to my copy of Blonde on Blonde—
Matt Kierstead in full Nazi uniform on the stairway
to Audrey Stone, the girl I had a crush on:
"I'd like to machine-gun you up the ass."
Matt was so hip he liked the New York Dolls
and Iggy Pop, and stood for hours in train-yards
recording the serial numbers and the times

of every train that entered or left the yard.
His English father took us to the Newton mall.
Now no one has heard from him in thirty years.
One night we boiled all the chemicals in the kitchen
and poured them steaming from a pot on the hoods of cars.
Fifteen years later at the Christmas revels
we thought we were going to revive grand opera.

7. Landis and Robin

Landis came back from the dead.
In an empty swimming pool we saw his grave,
a museum display of radiant glowing jade.
He admired it long. "In life I was
too filled with self-loathing to perfect my art
until you found me at the very end."
And I: "You were the same man that you were then,
but never knowing it, till the time was ripe."
"You conquered the world. So little as it meant
when Cinderella was Cinderella again.
I had to take my life. I couldn't understand
the poems I wrote, Ben, not at all."
And I: "Tell me, are you happy where you are?"
"Oh, yes. Everyone is very friendly here.
I am taken well care of,
though I haven't begun to write."
Then turning, his face in darkness in the sharp light,
"Call Robin," then turning, then he disappeared.
For the better, I hoped. "Call Robin." Then I awoke,
but didn't. Two days later Robin was dead.

Monsieur Barbary Brecht

Who shall it fall upon to inspect
the comings and goings of Anthony Hecht?
The Cummings and Boeings, the strummings and knowings,
the summings and flowings of Anthony Hecht?

Maybe the Master, the shepherd and pastor,
the leopard, lean, faster,
that peppered forecaster,
the Phoenix and Castor, Monsieur Barbary Brecht!

Who will exhume the intelligent wanderings,
the diplomat, coup de tat, government squanderings,
and furious ponderings also that stem thereof,
and fonder things, of the late Howard Nemerov?

No one more furious, curious, serious,
sometimes delerious, always imperious,
mighty ambiguous, slightly conspicuous,
Jane Geoffrey Simpleton—Monsieur Barbary Brecht!

Who will expose as verbose the rich prose,
will deface and erase its slick surface with grace,
will unweave what he wove, and enclose what there flows,
of the flaws of the prose of Ernest Fellose?

No one more hounding, more pounding, more counting,
more hunting, or cunting, or brushed up with bunting,
than that master of everything Asians depict,
and the roots of all madness—Monsieur Barbary Brecht!

Actually what is it, I'm trying to say,
tomorrow, tonight, yesterday and today,
intangible, frangible, Monsieur John Mandeville,
irreversible, curseable, not nearly nurseable,
something appealing to Barbara Hutton,
I'm trying to turn myself off, but I can't find the button.
I tell myself, you should be more circumspect,
for one who's the houseguest of Monsieur Barbary Brecht!

General Walker inspired a stalker,
who hired John Pauker to be a big talker,
in Dallas with Alice, with much forethought malice,
his background they checked and they checked and they checked.

And though it was hot, and he took a pot shot,
played his part to the hilt, revealed nothing of guilt,
even when questioned by George Mohrenschildt,
who had made him defect?—Monsieur Barbary Brecht!

There are two different kinds of fuck.
The fuck that's fucked, and the fuck that's fucked.
And in Algeria—last time I checked—
both were reserved for Monsieur Barbary Brecht!

Professor Pitkins had a real tight jaw.
Perhaps he even wore a metal bra.
But if he did the one who could detect
that this was so was Monsieur Barbary Brecht!

If you see W.H. Auden you might just have boughten
a diversion, a version, a red and dread sturgeon,
a false bill of goods, and you may have been tricked
by that master of everything which has been bricked,

64

the one they call mother—Monsieur Barbary Brecht!

But apart from this world, where the great winds are whirled,
and the towers are darkened, childs play
with primordial knowing of Hindoos and fairies
and Edmund St. Bury's, and all that's most out of the way—
they may dig holes to China, or reveal their vagina
(in the hall suits of armour compelling good karma)
but no matter how darkness betray
the extent of the world, or the word, they have trekked
through inversions of Monsieur Barbary Brecht!

The ghost in the wainscot is trembling and bludgeoned
and wrapped in a fox that is dry and curmudgeoned
but the thespian sheets fly aloft in the air
and although there is tea, there is nobody there.

There is no one to draw lines with pen and with ink,
or to stain with hair coloring half of the sink,
but the wrought iron is animated, and the architect
of this elaborate absence is Monsieur Barbary Brecht!

Try typing his name and you might go insane,
at the way the hands work towards each other and then
go in circles repeating again and again
one insistent motif like a tom-tom refrain,
and then spiral upwards—an enigma machine
couldn't do it the justice of how it is whacked
on a simple corona—Monsieur Barbary Brecht!

In the hall the rich children glare and they stare
at the poor little visitor who enters there,
his musical prodigy greater than theirs

sends them scuttling in snide little groups up the stairs.
But the hostess is compassionate and hands him a score,
but he just doesn't feel up to play any more,
and wonders what lies behind the magnificent door
where the children all vanished, and his vision is flecked
by the shadowy mustache of Monsieur Barbary Brecht!

If I were a 1926 model Ford
I would carry your body and then I'd have poured
it over the bridge and into the river
without so much as the least tiny shiver.—
So the love letters of little girls run
but they never have ever so nearly much fun
as the brain that delights behind eyes that reflect
the abductions of Monsieur Barbary Brecht!

It is Christmas time and the world is still
and the windows like lenses of glass that are cracked
where the presents are stacked on the shelves do not kill
the spirit of our saviour who's come from afar
for whom the child left the door slightly ajar
the deciduous rustle of Hyperborean pines
shuffles in the three wise men and the brilliant star shines
and no one, but no one could ever detect
the immaculate presence of Monsieur Barbary Brecht!

The spires of Mem Hall, and what's trapped in the cat,
like the great North wind go this way and that,
and no matter how anyone's ever detained
by a shivery feeling, a vague sense of what's stained
by what came before us, or what's not yet come,
there isn't a formula for doing the sum,
yet all of your queries you might kindly direct

to the highly compassionate Monsieur Barbary Brecht!

The fire's last flicker as it falls in the shadows
leaves all in the darkness of its afterglows.
The winter winds whistle, and somewhere a thistle
is lodged in a crevice of snows.
Mother and father, sister and brother,
the family's together, and all will protect
the spirit of Christmas, and sing the great missal,
in the translation of Monsieur Barbary Brecht!

Behind every brick there's a visual trick,
an encapturement that's luminoso,
in the rain, in the brain, in the strain, in the wane
of enrapturement, tres furioso.
It's a kind of a click, that may not or may stick,
and may trap what I meant, I suppose so.
Like back issues of old magazines might reflect
a spectrum of tissues—Monsieur Barbary Brecht!

Dante and Berryman, and Bernard Herriman!
All can be found here, can be seen in sound here!
It makes no difference what order, what corridor,
except as causation's perceived as sensation,
no border can thwart or export or condense here
or give any quarter to the immense sense here
of Nemerov, Tamiroff, Bellow or Hecht—
all one, the domain of Monsieur Barbary Brecht!

So tell me, just how if they are indivisible
we need them. We seed them when they are invisible!
The order they cede to is perfectly cracked.
Call in the correctives—Monsieur Barbary Brecht!

The films of the forties, the great women's films,
are baked on the surfaces of post boxes and kilns,
like the whisper of porcelain, the threads of empire,
that visit the sky and retire in a spire,
they expire in the senses, for one and for all,
one vast waiting ocean, the windows recall,
with curtains and windowseats holding hopes checked,
but nothing's arrived today—Monsieur Barbary Brecht!

The Alps

Over and over again brick windows rise
like signs of permanence into the skies—
they wash the windows dusty with disuse
which individually although abstruse
invoke the thousand clotted celluloid
of Charlie Chaplin or of Harold Lloyd—
the ones who come here are very few
but they do what they have come to do
in little gestures and in little words
not knowing ever what they're climbing towards.

Interlinearly in swastikas
that bring to mind old Baedekers
brick windows stop each wandering eye
and gulls that climb into the sky—
how can we know that they are real?
That they impel beyond what we feel
the clotted plains of blood-swept snow
resounding a long time ago
as though still news? Or what we see—
a technical magazine, a cherry tree,
a single bird, the rain exploding like a sea?
And how far back would one have to go?
The sea beast and the death at sea are slow.

2

The first Freud in the first wood
has also like us understood

that what emerges from far away
has only come to go away.

And the thick flood upon the floor
is signifying nothing more.
The piles of interlocking angles rise
always as if to put their stamp upon the skies.
But those who from a distance come
fail to resemble they are home.

The simple steams in private eyes
are real, rerecognize surprise.
Apocalyptic shapes in piles,
original as we surmise.

3

Yet here, in these Alps,
where each one is a stranger,
where no one senses danger,
there is no need to hold a door
with a vacant eye, disturbing the mountains.
The floorboards clog, but will be dry
when the spring comes. Or is it spring?
Each one turns the latch, and lets it swing,
each in his sweater makes the floor grow wetter,
each thinks that he is better.
And the math problems go unsolved.
Yet each one is resolved,
with his senses closed, his face close to the paper,
and the pen scurrying, the heart burying
the look of each stranger, through the door hurrying,
resolved to solving problems with no end,

let no man say that this one is his friend.
When the spring comes
the Colombian Greek or Russian Spaniard
gesticulates wildly, blocking the cafe floor,
and the black countess is in love with him no more.
What has she to lose?
She titters wildly like a goose
and though her eyes pop wide
she doesn't see the man in mocha brown
who stands in the door, looks up and then looks down.
And why should she complain?
She, who has been numb too long for pain,
who doesn't notice there is any strain.
And no one here has cabin fever!
The most lost one is like an eager beaver,
asking to be called Tiresias.
Even through restraint they make a fuss,
saying—you are one of us.
But I, I drink my coffee and scan my paper,
alone I see the man in mocha brown,
and though I have no sense of any caper,
I watch his eyes look down,
and wait for the entire afternoon to taper.

4

And now my story of one of the others.
How, in a cleft of never seen again,
this witness yet repeated, that which exists in possibility.
That it should be seen thus, here, captured by four walls
and never to move—the echoes so resounding.
To see it so is to say it must have been thus.
There is no utterance for recognizing

that these, too, swim towards a completion,
never to come again, but to be always.

5

Who but the least of them can give assurance
that to exist—to radiate out of a name—
is to form a decahedron, in which
the wars of history are foresworn
for the sake of a pure principle,
a stellar mountebank of guidance.

So it was—coming out of the theatre,
where the least desire had been crowned a king,
and no one looked to see spring was returning,
for the shadows of intrigue and ambition forbade it—
the sole cardinal announcing like a trumpet,
a silver Buddha or toy elephant,
sang without voice of a unique recurrence,
and stopped once at the top of the opera stair:
that these too have no name, yet, unassailable,
exist to tantalize their lost forbearers
with a sense that they too must have been.

Come up here, come up out of the stair.
Enclose me as you open this last package.

They made it so, and ever it will be thus.

6

Who like one rising subsisting in the morning,
turned out, also departed them.

That he should rise to see one whitest icon
as if preserved through all the tumult of dreams
to fail only to catch his eye only.
What if she has gone, and left no name.
Only the sense of her exists in him,
peopling the unpeopled towers.
She will not come again.

7

What we have in common is poetry.
That it should take this form.
Snow piles. Signs of spring. A rainy wind.
Now and as always through the dark corridors
trying beneath the levels of the sky
to find this garden, and a little forgiveness.

It is impossible, but should traverse
the opposing hope, as a pedestrian
crosses one coming along where he is going,
fusing along one line since it was snowing,
to veer out towards what the circle represents.
All the oblique obstruction of these laments.

8

Pounding, pounding, pounding, the blood of the king,
the long torches flaming and thundering.

What did the headlines broadcast?
The shapes of construction, but in one stable form—
as if the white edged page were one vast sea
existing long, but only known for being told.

For the virtue and the edge of modernity
are the capacity for larger myths
endlessly repeatable—so blue eyes blare
not only the milk horns, or the garden's hedge
but the vast sea that slays the sword
as if a thousand thundering heard
quite far away, had jumped instantly and voicelessly
on one vital truth—as dark and drowning
as the first storm that blew apart the mountains.

Imperial they jump, with swords between their teeth.

At the Tabuki Kabuki

She was a hothouse flower, but she grew
to such proportions that she never knew
her brand of people, less her brand of steeple,
and saw things as they happened, from the view.

Her husband took her on his trips to Asia,
to count the factories, and meet the heads
of government and business. In her beds
were flowers, chocolates, cinctures of aphasia.

In time the path sloped upward, and the driver
relaxed a bit, began to tell his story.
It grew less clear just who was driving who,
she, the loquacious one, or he, the taciturn McGiver,

or if it was a modern sort of dory.
As she listened, she began to rue
the little fables, and the many tables,
and the entire vast illusion, too.

New South Wales

Splendid the glorious technicolor gales
that break the unbreakable spirit in New South Wales.
All tends towards dawn, but night is strange and long,
plays out a drama where there's something wrong
that's never said. The green balustrades
are freely entered by too well trusted maids.
The carelessly worn inscription at the approach
to the manor is a mildly forbidding reproach.
The table's set for six deceptive men
who drink together and remember when
they all were younger, fates were sealed in anger.
The shabby port which doubles as a border
tries to preserve some semblance of royal order.
The governor bathes, is briefed on each new stranger
holding some parcel of land with his fierce will.
True friendship survives the time it learned to kill.
The sobbing of the old life's worn bud quails.
A chrysalis is born in New South Wales.

Hell's Angels

Three Oxford chums, but one of them was German,
before the war, with April blossoming
and the bright futures, subject to the king.
Now paired to death, uncompromising quota,
defensively aggressive last iota,
he swooned and realized he was his sister,
fired one last shot, as if he would have missed her.

Yet she who was identical to he
had grown alarmed when he first raised the curtain
on his obsessions, all the mad possessions,
that he had laboured to withhold from her.
What did it matter if his friend aver
her beauty or authority to judge
the same as he, that troubled him so much.
Why did he wish to save her from exposure
to his own doings, which in life they touch
as if in death, no closure overmuch.

And so it was for him she took the bullet,
although he were the only one to feel it.
Darkness prevails, but somewhere it is bright,
and somewhere his friend thinks of her tonight.

Desert Song

After all, it was a simple thing
to concentrate attention in the air
to where new-budded flowers filled the spring
with deference, desire, and with care.
The desert must have been a beautiful
excursion, hot winds blowing in her hair,
with scents to carry back to where you will
the evening moments, classical and still;
throbbing, such revelations as you dare.
Mark thus the twain, so immanently torn,
as to deposit gazes on the sill
where all is glass, beside a double moon,
where both the past and future are outworn.
What is that jingle, some insipid tune,
cavorting through the melody of words,
and should the morning come too blessed soon,
what inquiry could be put to the birds
that harbour light, corrupt these formulas
that splay what is, disfiguring what was,
in the event, relinquishing the cause.

Crisping the Comedian C

And with my sword cane I rapped the dog on its head.
To its master I said:
"The soul's expanding to make room for you
among the piles of rusted bric a brac
that make men grimace, revile themselves in church. . .
I felt the ground beneath begin to lurch,
increased my laughter with its rolling waves
laughter increase. . .
as he lunged forward trying to save himself. . .
I was an honest man. What could I do?
I pushed him forward where the great vacuum grew
and marvelled as he fell. . .
into the silence of the pits of hell.
"That's one less editorial to write,"
I thought, and blinkered to recall the light,
and blinkered to recall the blight. . .
the scourge of man. . .
I like to help them any way I can.
In my emotions not a thought of man. . .
but that his docile sudden-widowed wife
might serve the lord. . .
replace, with some improvements in accord
with justice and increase, a missing life. . .
I dyed my hair.
A most enticing shade of emerald green,
and knowing the precise dimensions of her lair,
(and its location)
I took me there. . .
in search of satisfaction, and a queen.
She was the best damned thing I'd ever seen.
I smiled to mechanize my spotless luck.

As we proceeded...
no human call we heeded...
I do not think that men will speak to me.
But wider, wider, like a churning sea
of foaming lavender and sapphire green
I met my match...
How can the blameless blame me for my snatch?
I laughed to see
that God had spread his vistas out for me,
his servant lord,
no matter how much I murdered or I whored...
I was quite sane.
And turned to mark my profile in a pane
of ice that served my child-bride for a heart...
She promised a new start...
and I was wondrous, seeing how I'd changed;
the souls of men were cobbled there and ranged
across the germ of my experiment...
But at the crack of dawn these visions went,
and I was back among the human race;
answering servants in my modern palace...
though one thought, ordinary, flamed and flitted
of how my research proofed that I had fitted...
and I was not incognizant of place...
answering letters in unbridled solace...
an evening like a fortnight had them piled
and crumpled on my desk...
Although I cannot, I afford a smile...
and set out half a mile...
My soul was stirred, and hungered to be reviled,
revived and furnished...
where the creature's dignity was burnished
on all she touched...

I bowed my head. My emerald locks she brushed. . .
grew wiry and strange...
yes, in that glass I recognized a change
of heart. She wept and promised a new start. . .
But how can I begin. . .
A child sees vistas in the hammering rain,
and does not ask if everything's the same. . .
one night I fell. . .
and nothing shall restore me to His Grace.
Yet in its infancy the new-born face
is pocked and filed. . .
and strangely familiar. Something in me smiled.
It's hard to find a perfect spot of shade. . .
Life is the best thing that I ever made. . .

In the Garden

"I'm furious with you!" she shouted, pushing him off the bench.
All pivots, emblems that ordered the circulating stars
amassed one throbbing ember, scintillating, sparked
by his learning, all he had yet of knowledge.
The true bridegroom bent in the mulberry stalks
at evening. Embers crowded on each stalk.

October Elegy

Well all those leaves don't truly give a shit
when like a pauper's race the market lines
of carts go sailing backwards through the wind
and blood stirs colder, closer to its home,
to settle in to darkness...
Pierrot's white face is just one souvenir
you took to try to stay upon the wall
of idle blood men of whose family
you sturdied eyes against as to recall...
now who shall know, when walnuts breathe and ape
the derelict saturns of the wind-torn grape
or amplify
stern ape-like warnings of a muscled sky...
these are not the same, and yet they are,
racing down blood paths clotted with dry leaves
and synthesis, for no one to please...
as if at last arriving who you are.
The expected one. Frank Hamilcar.

A Night in Claremont

When the wind goes down, and with it night
surrounds the elementary, fantastic gardens—
idling a moment in recess from the crowd
by Byzantine fountains studded with night jasmine—
your talk of Shakespeare burdens deciduous leaves
trembling the shadows where I wait
for variants with sterner variation,
peppering the icteous footstep's pause.
Blown through with visitorious tremulations—
veritably keen, they publish a rumoured text
long caught among the leaves, the horns and bramble—
I wait it out, drinking the air's shrinkage.
My old reprobate of blasts and Stambouls,
carries a sorry cane. For him night's gin,
but I am young as any promises,
colliding with the imperious speculum.

Clock

The hero moves like clockwork in two parts
that fade and then reverse in shocking light
before passing into stunned eternity—
how could he be so cool playing two parts
a subject of two kinds of analysis
saying goodbye but leaving only once
objectifying the world's phallacies
exposing the roots of his paralysis
as bright or even brighter than his guide?
She is the one who has no need to hide
her faith in him—the border of a wraith
whose is the order of undoing death.
Two parts converge in passing through the stations,
the porter weds their panic with their patience
like a clock's face, the stillness in the motions
of the clock's hands—the running of the sands
observes the hour figure of the glass
each of the two times the coupled heroes pass.

Gethsemane

You were insane, and I was sane,
now you are sane, and I'm insane.
I met you first in Gethsemane
when you are gone, and I remain.

The gardens there were lightly flush
at introduction of your blush
the kissing shadows nightly touch
time shadows render from the flesh.

The very bushes seemed to move
with attitudes approaching love
at the last moment to reprove
as if they didn't want enough.

Where earlier entering the town
calm was embedded in reknown
(directly it descends from this
perfect betrayal of a kiss).

The stirring petal on the bush
ignited by the kiss of flesh
the fragrance stirring in the air
shimmering like a distant star
the evidence that you are there
though even now it seems so far.

When you are gone, we meet again
when like a shadow fame and name
are predictably the same.
Men view the son, the desert plain;
when you are gone, we meet again.

The Imperialist Goes to India

Hey, you look just like your facebook photo.
No, you don't! I read your pores like a map
of everything that's wrong with the world,
plus everything that's right. Fields and fields
of daffodils and roses and poppies extending
all the way to the edge of the unshorn
virgin territories unexplored by balloon.
What is the word for this? It wells up
like silence in my groin and chokes
up in my throat like consonants
depleted of syllables. Ooooooooo
then nothing. I sit by a roadside
and have my fortune told. My lines speak triumph
but the voice that cloaks them is ominous.
I may have left Omaha and Idaho
to come to this, but I have fallen in love
and will not leave this till death wrenches me.
Like a librarian without a library
my love shines, she is loved by everyone!
Even small animals adorn her Madras
silks, would gladly die for her.
She cleans her perfect teeth with poppy seeds
and looks on me with a pure look of love.
What is it I see on the other side of myself?
I see, I see, a thousand monkeys
looking through a glass that separates
me from you—I see you trying
to penetrate the glass, but I can't hear your words.
What are you saying? This drama is intense,
too much is swarming over the old castle walls.
Is this what my aunt meant back in Omaha?

Believe in yourself. Do what you love.
I thought that I had power, held the strings
to my own destiny, and those of others.
Or is this all a dream, will I awake
to find I loved what I already knew.

Honolulu

We arrive in Honolulu. The mail carrier
expels us on to the tarmac. Coconut palms
smile investigatingly. The vista expands
as we emerge from motion. A taxi shuttles
us goggling through narrow towering hints and glints
of what's to come. Magic acts of checking in
to the hotel are a concealed transformation.
A telephone that watches a pool from the window
and waving sweeping palms like a transmission.
Then we are truly here. Alone at last. No one is following.
We shuffle quicker to get a little distance.
Now there is nothing between us and our desire.
The sky is personal. Even the natives
might mistake us for people with a purpose.
We move along in shuttering episodes
of patience and impatience, waiting for night to fall,
we guess. The coconuts grow darker,
and something leaves us, identity, inhibition?
It filters out diffusing us in waves
where the old calendar confirms a machete,
stopping the blood in our ass, flat cold and hard,
white flotillas of designer words
dying like a fever, over and over.
The sky like a flag unfurls and flaps
in darkness like a drunken midnight football.
Everyone's left. The past regains
its grip on the imagination.
The frayed loose ends of wars
interfere with weddings. A moment's headline
watches like a byword, a foreign detective.
The cream of youth, the best of a generation,

gathers in silent reticence and white slacks
around the gladiolas at the luau.
Each romantic grove chained to the coast
adapts its own periphery, identical
to any that drops into oblivion,
repetitive branches of mechanical production
the salt foam laps in coral depths of darkness,
glittering bones that blast forgetfulness.
(A reason to procure and expand casinos.)
A periphery that shrinks numb from sensation,
a few words teletext a generation,
then shrink like leaves in laughter, shimmering surf
exonerating rows of duplex balconies.
Buttering intimacy, esoteric solace
of a few logs, a few skittering sparks
like fireflies, a goat's skull.
Like pressed lapels, poker-faced, compare notes
and never enter the governor's palace.
The high bay rows
of honeysuckles like a maze,
like interlocking patterns each one shows
each one how he will pass the coming days
and nothing throws
the echoed rumours of this paradise
out where a hidden anchor glows and knows.
Each lives on maize and coconut milk
far from the submarine that hauls its silk
and the rich portraitures of empire.
I hear them faintly in the steel guitar,
and wait for the horseless carriage of dawn's fire.

Amateurs

Here as elsewhere most are amateurs;
secret agreements codify the flowers
the test pilot is killed by aviation
and the terrain obstructs negotiation
irrigation is misunderstood
and the first timers subject to the flood
the architect's design is never seen
but intersecting spirits stand between
the opposing and attracting signs
by which men know the mountainous outlines
the proud boxer's rubbed out by the mob
and the victorious emit a sob
even the greatest lawyers improvise
where there is often no room to revise
presumptions compartmentalize the rains
immersions curve at the dissolving margins
the landscaper externalizes purpose
which may be met or objects may oppose
with a due violence the unstated wish
that afterwards the clear signs may astonish.

The Strawberry Blonde

Miasmal afternoons in run-down shade
of clutter and rickety porches, smells of sex,
and filthy carpets, loose floors, leaning walls,
interminably appointmentless and stale,
in summer we holed up in a quiet street,
you graduated from Harvard, me with no course,
Hart Crane reborn, you were obsessed
with The Mountain Lion, with Boston Adventure,
we smoldered in some vision of the past,
green broken bottles shining by a fence
beat up and weather worn, dreams of sailors
drunk on leave, and stifling with beer,
sweating the heat, lagged on a sagging couch,
springs broken and collapsed, the curtains drawn,
and saw receding from my distant childhood
an old film I'd loved from fifty years ago,
The Strawberry Blonde, a vision of the past
itself, set at the turn of the century,
in which James Cagney tried to keep the girl
well at a distance, a shocking suffragette
who knew no bounds, whose eyes had lit on him,
stirring strange oppositions in his soul.
But she was true, and quite beside herself
gave up a little of her shocking ways
until he cursed himself for being hooked.
And yet they married, and lived long happy days.
Not so for us, who fought like cats and dogs
all summer over sex, over illusory slights,
hysterical, till we went our separate ways.

Forties Movie

I watch but do not relive the movie . . .
Bob Hope debarking for the primitive island . . .
This once engrossed me so much I couldn't sleep . . .
but followed him as if he were myself . . .
romancing the passenger sent to report on him,
beautiful in her white forties linen suit
with matching suitcases that brought him to her stateroom...
I could have kissed her, and wished he would for me . . .
Each wooden totem mask hiding watching eyes,
or slit eyed portrait in the abandoned castle,
caused him to stumble, never missing a wisecrack . . .
The island's spooks were only a criminal gang . . .
To put them out of business his discovered reason
for making the girl reporter want to marry . . .
I watched a commercial, and waited for the next movie . . .

Sylvia Sidney

They go on tap dancing. They go on and on and on
marching evening into night,
marching winter into summer.
My head swims and my points of reference
seem somewhat altered. Nothing stays the same,
so how then can I go on existing?
The summer rain, if it would ever come,
would prove these things are solid, of subsistence.
But as things are, with Madame's theatrical school above,
the air dry, and the piano needing to be tuned,
and nothing but these stale few days old crumbs,
I can see no hope, can see no future.
I wouldn't disturb anyone with this torture
if I were just to see if I could fly . . .

Abbott and Costello

Abbott and Costello, reporters at the hospital.
They wait with their cameras strung around their necks,
nearly in matching suits and hats,
while the nurses wheel patients on dollies back and forth,
up and down the halls. A blinking blonde in a white cream suit,
smart wide-brimmed fedora, her purse slung over her shoulder,
and a pouting expression of lovely street-wise grace,
waits to scoop them, suspecting they are dumb,
which they are. Lou with his simple manic joy in life,
impaled with worry, shy endless resourcefulness.
Bud with his careful, contemptuous certainty,
though usually careless and duped, sometimes correct.
A fast-talking numbskull who's painlessly done time,
and sneers his words, is in with the blonde,
or so it seems. Their action appears backstage.
No one knows it, but Lou is the fount of life.
He's never complimented, or rewarded,
except by a slick-talking conman easy to see through,
or a slick-talking banker glad to have saved his bank.
In just one movie, the sympathetic blonde,
or boyfriended brunette, has real love for Lou.
It's magic to see them sitting in a tree,
perpetual ghosts who wait for their release.
Abracadabra her magnetic horny trance,
the gangster's moll, or modern good-looking girl,
in another film, in another, and another.
The Scots clans round the mountain, shooting at them,
in plaid shirts making breakfast in the caravan,
vacuum salesmen visiting their lost niece.
The boyfriend will thank them, and always gets the girl.
Outside, the wind's hush stirs the mountain resort,

though far away, and is always revealed,
as wordless as birds, as the world's huge library.

Deep Sleep without Reservations

In my dream, I returned to Harvard Square.
A night on my own. I wanted a good meal.
I went to where I had often gone before.
It might have been The Pheasant, but it wasn't.
I was the first in line inside the door.
Some other folks came in, were quickly seated.
I mentioned this, and was brought to a table
in the large dining room, not the exclusive
(which had been heightened like a pedestal).
Three haughty men were seated at my table.
I asked if I could possibly sit alone
(I noticed there were many empty tables).
I tried to read the menu, but I couldn't.
I had a lot of questions for the waiter.
I waited for him, but he never came.
The people who came after me were eating.
I pushed my books a foot away from me.
I caught someone's attention, and complained.
I was told they would be with me shortly,
a party coming in had to be seated.
A hundred kids in matching uniforms
of red and white, with red scarves at their necks.
The people who came after me were gone.
I was enraged, asked for the manager.
She focused her preoccupied attention.
I told her I had been there many times.
I had to meet my wife and mother-in-law.
Was it possible I could order now?
A waiter would be with me in a moment.
The new waiter brought an Asian family
to join me, said she'd be back in a moment.

The child was feeding an enormous dog
she held upon her lap, just like a baby.
Bottle of milk in hand, she opened its mouth.
There I saw an entire electronic switchboard
of knobs and dials and indicating screens.
The young thing was a vegetable, they explained.
I nodded, and tried not to be too horrified.
Once again I asked for a new table,
rather politely. Suspicious and sick of me,
they asked me to stand and wait while they prepared one.
They seemed quite busy, perhaps disorganized.
The hundred kids in scarves were being served.
I'd had enough, and gathered all my books.
They brought me others I had left behind
on other visits which I had forgotten.
There were so many, how could I carry them?
I tried to stuff my pockets with the papers
I seemed to have left in a great trail behind me,
tattered bits of poems and telephone numbers
scattered everywhere. They brought me piles more books,
rare first editions, some books that were not mine;
some of these were multi-volume sets.
I found some others hidden behind a curtain,
where I recalled they sometimes had shown movies,
startled to realize how long ago that had been.
I saw the old projectionist hurrying forth
and disappear. I tried to pile the books
in both my arms, but they kept spilling out.
I got them balanced, and they led me out.
Just then, I saw that there were empty tables
in the daised and exclusive room.
In fact the entire restaurant was empty.
My hotel was across the street. I had ten minutes.

Couldn't I just order quickly, and be done with it?
They gave me a table. But now I had no menu.
All I wanted was a cornish hen,
something I'd had there time and time again.
I worried that they were remembering me.
Their manner now expressed extreme disdain,
as if they'd made their minds up to ignore me,
I was a particular class of mental patient.
I knew I wouldn't be going there again.
I woke to find I couldn't even breathe.

The Rain

I

And fill them they shall,
with cut glass, cut soap, cut candy,
down the cut shadows of the cut hall.
These imperiously not in thrall,
mix frivolity with rationality,
and ride the sea beams of the moon squall
out where the roofs are heartless and tall,
on orphanescent tides, as the rains fall
and break the solitude of each in his room,
studying madness or studying gloom,
to be whole, complete, the perfect bridegroom,
salient and unassailable, a deck of cards
to shuffle in the harmony of chords
that have no intention, and yet pursue invention
on its own terms, as gardeners consider worms.
This cataclysmic magic yet is tragic,
and shards the city in a billion lights,
effervescent, no longer concerned with rights,
but what the fool expends on solitude,
the partial perspectives of an interlude
without a channel, as love becomes manual
and rises aloft, as gingerly and soft
as the widest dreams of night air travel.

II

The sofas are covered and the old walls are plastered,
even the rain itself is duly mastered,
and a romantic attitude passed on,

in proper primness, and to each his own.
They sparkle there, the radiant miniscule
particles of light, of sadness, and of fright
that made them what they are, who sit and stare
and recommend an elder way of life,
ending in peaceful reflections of old strife.
The coverlets shall have much more to say
when night blankets the rain, and sums up all the day
into its pockets, drawers of contemplation,
where the old clock ticks out its steady relation
to what has gone. The rains go sweeping on,
reviving the laughter of a far distant youth
that yet remains, as constantly it stains
the outlook and suggestions of concentration,
imprisoned by old beliefs, struck on no reefs
of high built walls or visitors to tea,
a time that settles to a shade of green,
to recruit once more from the old hills
the spirit that an old perspective fills.

Tecumseh

I

Afternoon, languid and mysterious,
although perceived from one of many places,
is small and intimate, is infinite;
its meaning is in what goes on forever.
An anonymous statue in an obscure park
wards a few visitors to its desolation,
sweet smelling in a sunburnt shady breeze.
Walls limit sight. A single cardinal
fills windshaken trees with echoes of its song,
scratching in space the flashes of its movement,
distracting one from black coffee on the patio.
Over the wall perhaps the entire world
in thousands of scenes of action form a pattern,
and many rest, or tinker about a house,
leaving their driveways, or to them are returning,
always returning to the simple thing they are,
each one themselves, a complex of emotions.
But all that's hidden, and what there is to see
are only a bird, the trees, the wall, the fountain,
where nothing happens, beginning without an end,
unless it's in a distance so far off
that the lush needles and the ripe red berries
are cut down, not what they appear to be.
Yet he who watches from an upstairs window,
turning a curtain back to make a view,
wholly resides in simple clothes and slippers,
constructing within a pattern of his own
to thwart the harmony of hours and minutes,
as if old printed verses, word on word,

piled up the swirling dust motes of the morning
and marked an incremental calendar
with thought and gesture, motive and idea,
the impetus for many simple tasks,
and idleness itself were mental riches,
not wasted outside the compass of a room.
But here by the wall, up close, where neighbors squander
pipings and flurries of sounds the morning swallows
in its deft languid anonymity,
nothing changes, associating time
with a scene like this, though many years ago,
the subject of the gardener's repetitive hoe,
and childhood's musings, words within a book
that's seldom taken down to have a look.
Silent and still, its roots go on and on,
smelling of rich earth, and a fresh cut lawn
where no one goes. Even the gardener
must leave us to this final meditation.

II

He led me out of the intellectual tradition
and into the back yard
where like snares of autumn, clasps of spring,
the foliage curled about his crisp dry words.
So much that has gone before
lies torpid on the ornate stone bench
that's flat as waiting . . .
for ideas the mind seems to recall
of what is lovely, what has never been.
But that unresolved and fluid flux
of his words, originating in
the laundry room next to the kitchen

(where brillo boxes billow a decade's tide),
has impregnated as some furious leaping star
will above the moon the night of the school play
an actress spherically on the astral plane,
to glow in gas-works, private scrapbooks, yearbooks,
not only each soul of the babysitting neighborhood
or lamp that lights each window like a magazine,
with her one image, wordless, disappeared,
struggling homewards, past a father's world
of chains of obeisance, chains of defiance,
is impregnated with the telluric time you are,
knowing only the idea, the concrete absolute.
So fire dwindles. But to harness birds
as stars, retrace a dream, convert
those lapsed impingements upon a code of hope
to express eternal music with indifference
is only love—in any myriad form.
So he—tired and absolved
kicked all the lined up matchsticks of his theory
into the laughing bottle of his door stoop
to know unkind—the sturdy marble hallway,
as whisked away by maps as calendars.
No one is surprised by his ideas.
This is tedium and is comfortable.
But all the lined electric shocks of brambles
share in the patchwork query of the bridegroom
go he by falter or fine default
into the garden for a moment to stretch his legs
and make of the gardener one simple request—
to return here at any rate, not be
too crowded by these people who rose the estate,
Their charm is harmless, but the flowers are great.
So—to one room, anent the museum city,

as always were the backtalk of their talk,
and blue and black and green—not shedding dirt
to illuminate the mind night's city.
To serve thus such a gap of pity
on its own terms, as was meant by this.
His nature—laughter and
fluid and grave as a babbling stream
on a fine morning separated by the mountains
from all of this, the laughter, the cool tea, the gingham
as red as time peers through the town parade
in glacial valleys petering through to brambles
to condense all conversation to one word.
He knows what he is talking about. Not all the others,
who call him crazy, an island where a remote
cache of codes and maps rusts in a metal box,
as vigorous as his language in the sands
that strand and striate through the soldier's nerve
to serve one buttered bun in Queen's hospital
and dismantle a theory, mount a collage
of newsprint, bivouac the observatory
expecting nothing but this dull response,
the same argument that the brilliant actress
shines illuminably above our dreams and hopes
tethering us to good witness, and for awhile
can expect us at the hour of service
to be not there, beside the bed, the scrapbook,
the white phone, the white blanket, the white floor,
the bright phone, a leather yellow of silk
to tie these notebook drafts,
the diary of a young debutante.
Life has its meaning. By the library
a brook ran. To get across
meaning, but stopped by the night

only to measure the utterance of the heart's flight.
These files are closed, but can be shown to you.
It was easy to help ourselves to art supplies.
I also am myself. I will do anything you want to do.
But think how the strings of nights
go gently masked as law to condone madness—
"paid for by the community"?
The reserve is so great on these things
that these themes are repeated.
The Nobel Prize is given to the young
in the name of elders who have ceased to matter,
except as they were intuited, long before we ever met!
Unbent and grotesque upon a beach
at night the played out light
played upon the essential right
of the drowner O shadow who you love so much,
as you yourself loom large, confirmed in the space program,
never paying dues, being yourself,
and no mould breaks,
there is no visitor,
he folds under his towel
and visits the dark wake
while you look on, out of the shadow
and hush the laughter of a sudden scholar
to delay a moment on the floor
till things get ripe and focused—

These sheets of sound, have pound for pound,
expended fields of pergoram
and quorum, for time must have quorum,
delay little upon a neutralizing machine
of inhibitions, or of planned vacations
stalked by the weeks that follow

in a small metro capitol.
It is encouraging to find yourself in a movie theatre
with no responsibility as a guideline or window
and hence the line curves, as a coastline toward the pacific
spectral maelstrom of our world.
Time is ripe for fiction, not of the novelistic kind,
but that which grows out of friendships on railways,
on tennis courts in exotic communities,
gated above rocky mediterranean cliffs.
Sun squeezes the morning sweat, the high mountain rises
and burns your cheeks, fair from being so dry
until the outer cursory fades with orange juice,
a family of calendars, erasers and memos
to exclude culture from his possible rebellion.
His triptych eyes rescind laughter with a smirk
or a dry snicker, a snuffle through the nose
I understood best, the silent classics of the forms.
They may be for each man, like a stamp collector.
And that is true. But what they couldn't get
he stood in little need of utterance of.
His plans are his forefathers'. They are bricks.
The women in green eyeshade welcome visitors
and those in the highest service get to relax
for this is harvest and the October augury
of tea leaves and of freshly creaking tile.
They are just glad to sit and eye each other.
And all stand helpless, partaking of the dead
at the hour that sets aside the weather.
There is no need to reduce this to indifference.
At any rate he tried. But failed successfully,
completing his philosophy, unspoken as it should have been.

Allegro quasi Largo

After the nils and ninnies, after the floating cities,
all this, and so much more . . .

The ghost of Landis tells the ghost of Robin
in the sample crypt where the trains stop,
where no one goes, where the light stops
to be deflected in the eyes as in life . . .
What are the means, on what is the way bent
that we stood here before without seeing.
The party climbs to meet the last peal of laughter
where the dream ends, where you speak no more,
awakening shuddering to stop vanishing.

The tiger hunches in the spectral jungle.
The littlest tiger primes his little sphincter.
Only the fronds wave, and the near shores are not far,
the water what is it, I do not wish to say.
Under that hotel roof, well blue and bleachy
after white cloth and continental breakfasts,
after the sea's tide and the afternoon swim,
and so much more . . . Is there a need to stay far
away from the source of comfort, from the bee's knees,
from the queen's fond look at five o'clock.
I do not think that I shall speak to them.

Analysing light in the far room
I beheld his gaze, interpreting
not such things as we had known
in the way we knew them, but, with the knees' cough
as they may be understood to be,
renaming them according to a formula

for the spelling of things outside of what they are.
This then is the queen's visit,
her absolute certainty its guarantee of absence,
nothing to tell her, nothing she missed.
While advertisements roar on
under the telling, breaking the analysed light.
How to promote an exchange from here to there,
a sure guide for exigencies maintained
is a real problem in a dreamed elevator,
too real to let go of all resemblances,
despite being unable to recall, to muster a name.
Why then we were what we were before,
only I didn't tell you, and you didn't guess,
but now in the aftermath of that black mass
there's little to be done but that assuages,
and the miner gets no rest, in the deep mine.
And the dinner gets no reply, and the dish languishes.
Clean up this mess, O Son of God,
the better that my speech approacheth wholly
the forms and conditions of a prior approval,
that calling card or palm sized circular
that goes away, to get so much work done.
As long as you work, says the rushed hysterical voice,
then, I don't have to sit here, arrogant, indignant.
Arrogant. Martin Kozinski
butters his skis with butter and flour.
Have a good time, they warn him, and so talk.
Have a good time, the neuron zero.
Parted before we met the dancing ladies.
The diurnal and indigenous binoculars
assert their existence, deny a crowded code
for crossing rooms in a jumble of sounds,
but silence is golden when the cat speaks.

Birds I guess. And finally blow off some steam.
"Alright." She says it like a threat.
Somebody does it, but she didn't do it.
I do not even know what she means
but as if the world turned, and it all came back,
I know where you are moving, circle around and come back.
Above all the will is extinguished
in the exercise of a consoling reticence.
Only the logical tiger makes sense.
There is no way out. Forgive it.

I'm stepping out for a smoke, but thought I'd see
if a package had been left for me in the basement,
or if that other, recounting so many statistics,
had come to order all my memory
as I had failed to do, when I might have.
His books are the only books I shall read,
from them extract a sense of the others as they could be,
as they shall be, if we ever meet.
It is no problem to rise to the street level
if for a moment to light a cigarette
and ponder the perambulations of shrieks in the air.
They tell me that I must go back to bed,
not to sleep, not even to be too warm,
but to receive these books revealed to me.
Hah hah hah hah! The Acapulco morning
lives in the heart's little cleft, in the train station
where I exchange a nickel for a bar of candy,
a meagre command for an executive,
lost easily enough in the drowning of paternal voices,
they drown so late, and steady like the sea.
Well then, shall you tell him?
Impossible to describe these stadiums

where the change took place, the heart became a man's
under the cover of the map's old colors.
They too roar, steady as if to replace
simpler languishings on thinner avenues
at the hour of darkness that recalls the dead.

Closed Space

Any positing of existence—any positing of anything, true or false, real or supposed—any positive assertion—any assertion—concludes an inhering whole posited by contiguity of underlying supposition not alien to itself. To conclude an alien entity would only in fact be to extend the underlying supposition to its positive limit. Yet to speak of a limit in this sense is only to refer to the inhering contiguity and continuity of all supposition—outside of which only not a thing at all can be subscribed. If its notness can be asserted or supposed it is then inherent in its ascribation to be contiguous with any selection of order whatever—supposed or not supposed. Supposition itself is a key to the inherence of all that is not supposed; there is no not supposing that which is not supposed in the act of supposition. The posited inclusion then—if any thing at all is posited—must inhere to a unity of form. Only one form is possible to enclose all that is positive within a background that is nonexistent: a perfect sphere which is continuous with itself; for otherwise to inhere in unity would be to continually radiate outwards from any point of inherence in every direction without cessation or end. By definition to continually progress in such a manner would contradict the inherent unity that would have to be essential even to any pattern amplified to an infinite progression. To posit infinity is contradictory to any positive inherence whatsoever. Being and existence by necessity inhere even in the most variegated and complex of possible patterns to an inherent unity which on any terms must be ultimately finite. The so called expanding universe is itself the most finite and unified of patterns or propositions. The only form which represents not shapelessness or non-ultimately unbounded extension is that which closes itself in a perfect bound or continuum: and that is by any extension of principles inhering in the finiteness of unity incapable of being expressed or formulated without bias except as a sphere. There is nothing outside of this sphere. Unity is a self contained proposition. The sphere merely represents the totality of all that is in any sense positive or possible.

That is to say that all curves towards its infinite progression towards itself.

II

In fact this sphere must be oblong in order to account/compensate for the variability implied by the division of things into their retrograde actions towards themselves—as a hermetic sphere could or could not take into account all changes reduced along a single curve. Roundness is all. The oblong spherical accounts for differentiation.

III

Although the star we are closest to is the sun, has no one ever noticed that there are vastly many more million light years on the one side of us than on the other side of us? If we travelled long enough in a straight line we would return to our starting-point, true, but the fact is that we are already at our starting point, and that we are closer to it on one side than on the other. That is to say that the time travelled is less than the time it takes to start to return.

IV

Conventions of Measurement

To plot any grid is to impose squares on any consecutive series of degrees projected throughout the spherical. Each square encompasses and engenders an infinite series of mimic perspective spheres within the finite spherical. Each gradation in each series in turn generates an infinite series of mimic perspective squares within the finite (oblong) spherical (in a sense obligated squares), such that every accountable square moves by the static guidance of its own mimic square.

$f = f_2 - f_2 / \{Vf = x - x16H\}$

V

In fact the earth is continually rolling like a somersaulting acrobat (or a set of chinese wheels) past a series of suns—night day night day night day night day—in a long progression—all seen from a bedroom window— back towards the original sun.

(You notice when you go out for a walk that you are returning.)

VI

If I let my fingers wander idly over the keys of a piano I might play a Beethoven sonata.

But even a Beethoven sonata is always returning to its source.

In fact every time I idly run my fingers over a keyboard I am playing a Beethoven sonata. In fact I am playing the entire set of Beethoven sonatas. And they are all returning to their source.

VII

In this Corner

The world is on fire. But we can see it.

Increasing organization beautifully turning.

VIII

How many flights since the inception of aviation? How many miles flown? Over what arc returning. An arced line relative to the earth's rotation. Relative to universal expansion. Now once again see—Paul Henreid and Ingrid Bergman taxiing out of Casablanca. The stars glitter. Conrad Veidt is removed to displace Humphrey Bogart to Claude Rains. [A five pointed star continuous as it is drawn.]

*

Refuel in Ireland to continue to Istanbul. Look out the window—only the stars are moving.

IX

Lights banging around over and over again—Scarlett O'Hara.

X

The Spittle Gatherer

People either look at you, or they look away from you. Caught myself wondering if the shrimp I saw tonight were from the ocean. If I myself was genetically engineered. Perhaps we've all been for decades. Secret that musn't come out, that's referred to by innuendo. Jack Parsons' parents came from Springfield, Massachusetts. My parents came from Springfield, Massachusetts. Idea of Pasadena, a genetic colony of culture. Two references in An American Chronology of Science and Technology in the Exploration of Space 1915-1960. Hugh L. Dryden, that's a pseudonym. You get to a certain point they're all pseudonyms. Made up entirely by a band of shareholders in the largest secrets. Massive eruption rocks the sun. What is the sun? Is it just fire, or is it a giant rock that's on fire? I think it's just gasses. Pasadena, I can see it like it wasn't there. Who told the flowers to stay on first? Massive eruptions all of the time. Who says opposition leads to growth or discovery? True opposition. Vote me out. Don't vote for me. Gregory Bateson and Derek J. de Solla Price. I think I know what they're talking about. Tibbets. Tibbets? You'd think they wanted us to get the joke. Patterned wallpaper to teach you stories. E=MC2. What is C? Hendrix! Like light that exists long before its sources, stars flying away from us as fast as they can go. We clink and then we drink. "And he was trying to say it was organic." I like to think of myself as a dead person, although I am not dead. Who on so important an occasion had surpassed himself by inverting the usual order of nature. Time moves backwards. It is getting earlier and earlier. Those movies of rice fields are our own idea of myth. Relatively recent. An hundred inch diameter mirror. Glass eight inches thick. Nine years to grind and polish. Gather enough light to register a burning candle 5,000 miles away. Some-one willing to go as far as possible into space, and just keep going. Carried by the force of expansion to the speed of light.

XI

An Old Lady in the Natural History Museum

And should the afternoon go down
upon the echo of the brown
enumeration of our race
and leaving a residual face
exempt us from this constant place
still see incognizant the sign
levelled between the smile and frown
and cropped hedge the long anodyne
and evening parallel they drown.

For there thin lips and watered eye
are hunched upon the citadel
in deep inversions of the sky
and permutations of the town
that the old crone will never tell.

XII

The Mahatmas

Cataclysmic simultaneity, how they return to the moment inevitable, too scary to face. Huge crescendo of volume to minor subtonic, then back again, a rock's face cliff, stark, sliding, struck by lightning, continually alternating, unbearable revelation. Shrouded in darkness, yet revealed. Horrible to look at. Those notes that are what you heard are now blinding. Yes, the expedition was sent to Brazil by the British. Like Dracula or the Mummy, they didn't even know what they'd hear. Elusive revenge of the gods, shaking the world, on a cliff's edge, stark (with lightning crackling, breaking the darkness). Ancient, not to be fooled with. Signals go out, received all over the world.

A blinding moon. Violence of subtonic winds, in Principe and Sobral. (The path of the eclipse.) She stands revealed. Unbearable revelation.

Too late. The Mahatmas sign their letters charged with electrons. (A decoded letter for every cigarette.) Decode. Decade.

I go to the corner then back again. Then to the opposite corner—the short private way. All at once, everyone comes out of their house.

We must have come from the sun.

(Private utterances reach me from a far way away.)

    *   *   *

When I leave, they all return to their houses.

    *   *   *

One of whom is on his way to his daily quiet work, and another on his way to denounce a fellow creature at the police station. (The piu piu bird speaks backwards to move forwards. Moonlight and streetlight splay the chlorophyl's spectrum. Only Havana turns the double agent. The logical tiger streams towards its objective.)

In imitation of the sun's energy—in its capacity of a direct motor. Forces at work in hidden corners of nature. Turning the Gunga or the Brahma-putra, back to its sources. View us as simple men.

Amritsur Nov. 1st [1880]

"not only that They existed". "given to Mr. Sinnett". "the Master K.H.". Avalanche in the Karakorum Mts. Letters will cease at her death. Simul-taneously in Tibet and Egypt, in London in Paris, in New York and San Francisco and Los Angeles. Russia and Prussia. Nearby in Peru. Principe. Breakfast is served in the Alps.

They have written, they have written. Written. Written.

Ben Mazer is the author of *Poems* (Pen & Anvil) and other collections. He is the editor of editions of the poetry of John Crowe Ransom, Frederick Goddard Tuckerman, and Landis Everson. He is the Editor of *The Battersea Review*. A graduate of Harvard University. and of the Editorial Institute at Boston University, he lives in Cambridge, Massachusetts.